A HOLOCAUST CURRICULUM

Life Unworthy of Life

**An 18-Lesson
Instructional Unit**

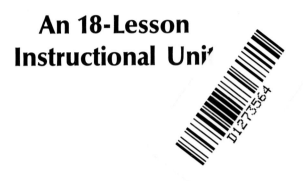

by
Dr. Sidney M. Bolkosky
Betty Rotberg Ellias
Dr. David Harris

Published by The Center for the Study of the Child

For further information or to place orders, please contact:

The Center for the Study of the Child
31000 Northwestern Highway
P.O. Box 9079
Farmington Hills, Michigan 48333-9079

TABLE OF CONTENTS

★ Priority Lessons
☐ Videotape

L E S S O N 1

The Destruction of Families and the Question of Personal Responsibility

HOLOCAUST CURRICULUM

THE H

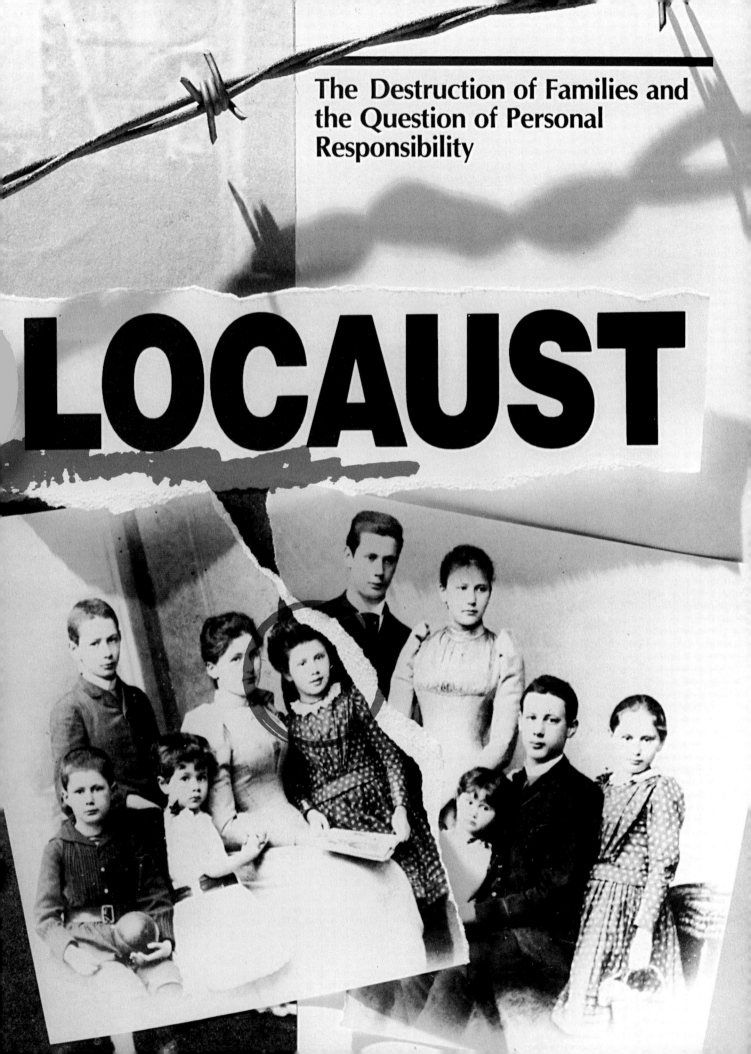

The Destruction of Families and the Question of Personal Responsibility

LOCAUST

There are no Readings in Lesson 1. Students will view the videotape "The Destruction of Families." A discussion will follow.

The Destruction of Families and the Question of Personal Responsibility

WHY STUDY THE HOLOCAUST?

Read each question first. Then, read the selection, "Why Study the Holocaust?" aloud. Finally, discuss the questions.

Questions

1. How is the Holocaust different from other mass murders or "genocides"?

2. What benefits can be derived from a study of the Holocaust?

3. In light of the comments on the video, what do you think the scholar meant by "After Auschwitz, anything is possible"?

The Holocaust is our legacy—all of us. It is essential that all of us understand what took place during the Holocaust. We live after and, thus, participate in post-Holocaust life. The tragic events presented in this unit of study represent one of the darkest periods in the history of the world. The Holocaust is over, but the nature of the society that carried it out exists here and now.

The Holocaust refers to the murder of some six million European Jews from 1933 to 1945. It was not the first state-ordained mass murder or attempted genocide (the annihilation of a people, nation or race). The first such attempt in the 20th century was the Armenian Genocide in which 1.5 million Armenians were murdered by the government of Turkey from 1915 to 1922.

The United Nations Convention on Genocide declared, in 1948, that genocide was "an odious scourge which has inflicted great losses on humanity in all periods of history." Since 1945, since the Holocaust, such policies have been conducted by several countries around the world against various victim peoples. Governments have embarked on courses to "freely exterminate" whole populations. The Pol Pot regime in Cambodia massacred hundreds of thousands of people between 1975 and 1979. During the 1967-1969 Nigerian Civil War, up to one million Ibos were killed in Biafra. In Uganda, between 1972 and 1979, over 75,000 people were slaughtered. Not only were political opponents murdered, but their families were also killed.

Genocide, the extermination of whole populations because of racial, national, ethnic, political or religious differences, has become almost commonplace.

Comparisons to determine which group suffered the worst tragedy serve neither the past nor the present. The uniqueness of the Holocaust, however, invites us to focus specific attention on it and its lessons for modern society. All the hallowed ideas and institutions of Western civilization have had to be reevaluated as a result of the Holocaust. "After Auschwitz," one scholar has written, "anything is possible."

This unit of study focuses on the murder of the Jews. The Holocaust differs from other genocides in several ways:

☐ The Holocaust was totally involving. Every realm of an enlightened, industrial society became entangled in murder.

☐ The Holocaust was not a barbaric undertaking. The killers used the most advanced technical, scientific means available. Places for the killing of millions were called death factories. Assembly-line techniques were adopted. Not only science but even medical science—doctors, surgeons, researchers, whole medical faculties—actively participated.

☐ Each step leading toward annihilation was approved by legitimate state authorities and was legally carried out by public officials. An elaborate system of human destruction permeated the courts, the diplomatic services, the police, the civil service, state legislatures and, indeed, all public institutions.

☐ Most civilians became indifferent to the destruction of their neighbors.

Perhaps, as a result of studying the Holocaust, you will be better able to identify the political, social and intellectual conditions which led to it. And, equally important, you may better understand how the Holocaust directly affected the lives of specific individuals. This unit may help you to see how the lives of people, some your own age, were and can be disrupted because of indifference and apathy.

By examining the behavior of civilized people, this study takes a painful look at how fragile morality, democracy and the sanctity of human life itself can be. The unit is designed to make us all more aware of our responsibilities to ourselves and others, so that, as one Holocaust survivor noted, "no such event will happen again, and the future will be safe for our children—for all children."

Reading 2B

THE STORY OF THE TWO NATHANS

Read each question first. Then, read the selection, "The Story of the Two Nathans." Finally, discuss the questions.

Questions

1. What are the similarities and differences in the two stories?

2. What might be occurring to some other teenager somewhere in the world at the moment you are reading this that is comparable to what Nathan C. in Kracow experienced?

On March 5, 1943, in a Midwestern city, the Jewish family of 18 year old Nathan C. worried about his late return from a date. His parents were concerned—he had not called, he might be hurt. Each moment brought them more anxiety. A neighbor walked by the house and they ran to the window. A car drove down the street and their hopes were raised only to be brought down, leaving them in deeper concern. He arrived late and was scolded. He had been delayed in traffic.

At exactly the same time, on March 5, 1943, the Jewish family of 18 year old Nathan C. worried about his late return. Each moment brought his parents more anxiety. Someone walked by and Nathan's mother wept when she saw it was not her son. A truck drove past their window and they cringed with fear. Curfew time came and still Nathan was not home. Their anguish increased. He had been seized by an SS unit on the streets of the ghetto in Kracow, Poland, and put into a forced labor gang. They never saw him again—he was beaten, shipped to a labor camp, and then to Auschwitz, the death camp, where he died in a gas chamber. His parents never learned this—they worried, and eventually, they, too, died in Auschwitz.

BASED ON A TRUE STORY.

QUOTATIONS BY PASTOR NIEMOELLER AND JOHN DONNE

Read each question first. Then, read the selection "Quotations by Pastor Niemoeller and John Donne." Finally, discuss the questions.

Questions

1. What does Pastor Niemoeller imply about speaking up for the rights of others?

2. What does John Donne mean by "no man is an island"?

Pastor Niemoeller (was imprisoned for opposing Nazi attacks upon the Christian religion):

"In Germany, the Nazis first came for the Communists and I did not speak up because I was not a Communist. Then they came for the Jews, and I did not speak up because I was not a Jew. Then they came for the trade unionists and I did not speak up because I was not a trade unionist. Then they came for the Catholics and I was a Protestant so I did not speak up. Then they came for me . . . by that time there was no one to speak up for anyone."

John Donne (the 16th century English poet and preacher):

"No man is an island, entire of itself; every man is a piece of the continent, a part of the main; if a clod be washed away by the sea, Europe is the less, as well as if a promontory were . . . Any man's death diminishes me, because I am involved in mankind; and therefore never seek to know for whom the bell tolls; it tolls for thee."

L E S S O N 3

The Aftermath of World War I: Germans, Jews and Anti-Semitism

HOLOCAUST CURRICULUM

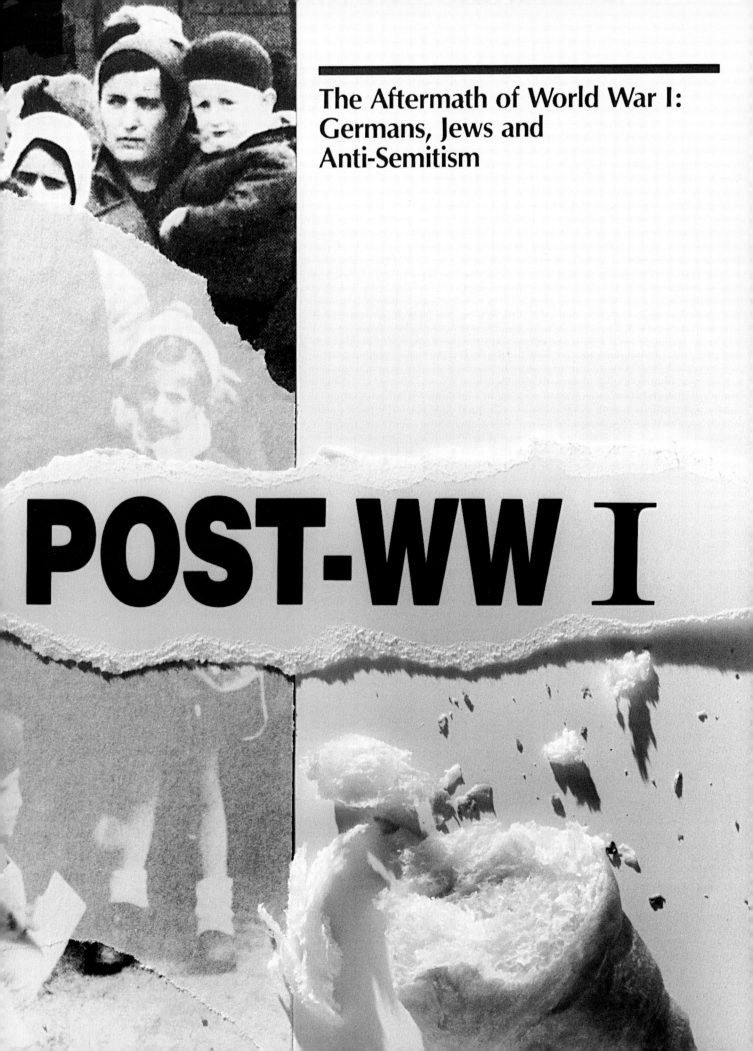

The Aftermath of World War I:
Germans, Jews and
Anti-Semitism

POST-WW I

CONSEQUENCES OF GERMANY'S DEFEAT IN WORLD WAR I

The consequences of Germany's defeat in World War I (1914-1918) were far-reaching:

☐ The old German monarchy, ruled by Kaiser (Emperor) Wilhelm, ended in 1918. The Weimar Republic, a democratic government, began.

☐ Inflation of monstrous proportions arose: for example, in 1910, a dollar was worth three marks. In 1921, there were one trillion marks to a dollar. One needed a wheelbarrow full of money in order to buy one postage stamp!

☐ Resentment and anger grew among many Germans who did not believe that Germany had really lost militarily because German troops still occupied parts of France and no foreign troops were on German soil. They believed that Germany had been betrayed at home or "stabbed in the back" by traitors who favored the new government. This notion became known as the *Dolchstosslegende* {*dolsh-shtoss-leggendeh*} or "stab in the back legend."

☐ In the Versailles Treaty, signed in Versailles, France, in November 1918, Germany surrendered unconditionally. The treaty demanded that Germany pay large amounts of money (reparations) to the Allies (France, England, the U.S.) over the course of the next 60 years. This was to cover the costs of the war, damages, and payments to widows and orphans of veterans, disability to the wounded, etc. It, also, gave German territory to France, Italy and Poland and saddled Germany with sole responsibility for starting the war. (The treaty was gradually changed in the 1920s and finally revoked by Hitler in 1935.)

The Austro-Hungarian Empire also was broken up. Austria, like Germany, became a republic and the nearly 700 year old Habsburg reign of the "Holy Roman Empire" came to an end as the Emperor abdicated (gave up the throne). Austrians, too, felt angry and alienated. Many Austrians and Germans felt they had been forced into democracy and resented it. The "good old days" of aristocracy and traditional etiquette were gone.

Summary: German society had been shaken to the core by the loss of World War I. Germans of all social and economic levels felt insecure, frightened, angry and frustrated. Many expressed those feelings by joining extremist political parties—either Communist or Nationalist—the two political opposites known as the extreme "left" and the extreme "right." As a result, there seemed only one point of agreement: no support for the new Weimar Republic. The government was, consequently, weak, lacking electoral and financial backing as well as prestige. The mood of the country seemed threatening, violent and depressed.

BRIEF HISTORY OF ANTI-SEMITISM

Questions

1. How did Jews maintain a community after being scattered throughout Europe?

2. How and why did the early Christians set themselves apart from other Jews?

3. How did some Christians view the Jews during the Middle Ages?

4. What were some of the differences between Christians and Jews in the Middle Ages?

5. How were Jews discriminated against during the Middle Ages?

6. What occupations were available to Jews as a result of this discrimination during the Middle Ages?

7. Why did Christians believe that Jews murdered Christian children?

8. What were some of the gains made by Jews during the 19th century?

9. What were some of the characteristics racists claimed Jews inherited?

10. How did people react to the belief that Jews inherited "rootlessness"?

11. Is there any historical evidence to support the myths of Jews as devils and murderers?

As a result of the conquests of their biblical homeland by Persians, Greeks, Assyrians and Romans, Jews were scattered throughout Europe. However, the Hebrew Bible created unity among the Jews even though they settled far from each other in very different cultures. They continued to pray in Hebrew, even as they took on the languages of the different host nations. They also continued to follow the laws and religious observances of the Bible. They carried with them their customs, religious rituals and beliefs.

At first, anti-Jewish feelings were primarily a religious matter. Christianity was a child of Judaism and considered one of its branches or sects. Jesus was a Jew who quoted from and interpreted the Hebrew Bible. Yet, the dilemma for early Christians arose from the refusal of other Jews to accept Jesus as the messiah. There had been Jewish groups that had accepted earlier messiahs. None of those groups, however, had broken with Judaism until this one. That break began soon after the death of Jesus with the teachings of Paul. He sought to gain non-Jewish followers for Christianity. Paul accomplished this by dropping the requirements of conversion: Christians would no longer have to follow the dietary and ritual laws of Judaism. He also abandoned the requirement of circumcision considered by Jews to be the biblical mark of the "covenant of Abraham." Paul's followers became the new Christians, separated from the parent religion, Judaism.

When the Jews tried to drive the Romans out of their homeland, the Roman armies destroyed the holy Temple in Jerusalem in 70 A.D. This dealt a crushing blow to the Jewish religion, as Jews were driven from their country and dispersed or scattered all over Europe. New Christian communities on the outskirts of the Roman world were unaffected by the destruction of the Temple. Their separation from Judaism widened even more.

Europe gradually became Christian through wandering Christian missionaries like Paul. In the 3rd century A.D., Christianity had achieved such success that it became the official religion of the Roman Empire. Jews were a small minority. They were considered foreigners and outsiders, strangely different. Some church officials even accused them of being agents of the devil.

The Jews continued their religious and social practices and, consequently, set themselves apart from Christian society. Christians were no longer instructed in the Hebrew Bible and often forgot the roots they shared with Jews. Jews persisted in praying in Hebrew, reading from right to left. Christians saw Hebrew as a collection of symbols having to do with witchcraft. Jews ate different foods and refused to eat what Christians ate, pork, for example. Christians saw these differences as mysterious and evil. Jews celebrated the Sabbath on Saturday rather than Sunday. Christians called this witch's or devil's Sabbath.

As they had for thousands of years, Jews practiced circumcision as a sign of their "covenant with God." Christians saw this as an evil custom somehow related to the sign of the devil. Eventually, Jews dressed differently. They maintained traditional customs, like growing long beards, while modern practice changed to shaving. Jews became stereotyped in their physical appearance.

Throughout the Middle Ages, local governments discriminated against Jews, denying them the right to own land or hold public office. Medieval unions (guilds) refused membership to Jews so that they could not work in many occupations. The effect of this prejudicial treatment and isolation was to force Jews into commerce, and many became merchants. Although the majority remained poor, some became wealthy. Because the Church prohibited money lending, Jews were among the first bankers. This historical condition would foster a stereotype of Jews as money lenders. That stereotype would increase persecution, especially in economically hard times.

From the 12th to the 20th centuries, Jews were persecuted, tried and murdered on the basis of many myths. The myth that Jews murdered Christian children, for example, was created in Norwich, England, around 1150 by a superstitious priest and an insane monk when a Christian boy was found dead. The boy was probably killed by an outlaw. The two clergymen invented the story that this murder was part of a Jewish plot to kill Christian children. The myth became more mysterious and complicated when the story that Jews required the blood of Christian children to make unleavened bread (matzos) for Passover was invented and added to it. Even some saints had supposedly accused Jews of murdering Christian children for their blood. Such stories spread across Europe and the Nazis would later manipulate them and other legends to stimulate racist anti-Semitism.

From the late Middle Ages on, anti-Semitism was expressed in many ways. Jews were expelled from cities or forced to live in restricted areas. Jews were excluded from various occupations and denied citizenship. However, in the second half of the 19th century, Europe became more democratic. The full or partial emancipation of the Jews was achieved in Prussia, France, England and other nations. This meant that Jews officially were granted limited or full civil rights by governments. Also, some economic and social restrictions were gradually removed by law. However, anti-Semitic feelings and beliefs lingered. Myths, superstitions and deep-seated beliefs still clung to Europeans and had become part of the fabric of their civilization. Occasionally, anti-Semitism exploded into violence.

The 19th century saw the beginnings of an anti-Semitism not based on religion but on theories that Jews were a separate "race." At the time, "race" meant a group of people set apart because of genetically inherited characteristics such as skin color. Some even believed that cultural characteristics such as beliefs, customs and behaviors were inherited by members of a race.

By distorting Jewish history, 19th century racists labeled Jews as wanderers who inherited their "rootlessness" through their "blood." Thus, their nature was determined by heredity and unchangeable. Wanderers were strangers; and as in the Middle Ages, people feared strangers. They saw them as dangerous criminals, wrapped in mystery and evil. Hate-mongers claimed that for the safety of Christian children, Jews had to be avoided. Or, better yet, they urged that Jews should be kept at a distance or driven out of Christian communities. There was no other choice—character was inherited, it could not be changed. Such a theory, pretending to be scientific, was adopted by Hitler and others who transformed theory to practice in the Holocaust.

Poor farmers and struggling urban people were suffering from the effects of the industrial revolution of the 19th century. Many lost their land. Many lost their jobs. Many lost their status and prestige. Worse, growing numbers of them could not feed their families or provide shelter for them in the new environment of the city slum. Nothing was certain any more. Some blamed their situation on the "rootless Jew" who became a scapegoat. They repeated the stories about the "rootless wandering Jew" and the ritual murders. They harped on the Jews as merchants and bringers of urban, commercial civilization.

Anti-Semites in the 19th and 20th centuries inflamed fear and hatred that had lurked beneath the surface. The myth of a world Jewish conspiracy was fostered by a notorious forgery called *The Protocols of the Elders of Zion*. This book claimed that the Jews of the world were plotting to take over the governments of Christian countries and, thereby, added fuel to the fire.

The myths and stereotypes of Jews were based on deliberate lies and ancient superstitions. It did not even matter if anti-Semites knew Jews who did not fit the stereotypes. Because they are based on irrational fear or resentment, stereotypes reject specific evidence. The real world does not matter when fear, superstition and resentment are at work.

With an ancient tradition of religious hostility to draw upon, racism brought together fake scientific theories and anti-Jewish stereotypes. It offered solutions to economic and social problems and promised a hope for a better future once the offending group was removed from society. Without critical thinking or questioning, frequently in blatant defiance of Christian morality, educated and uneducated people accepted the stereotypes and the mythology with terrifying results.

A definition of anti-Semitism might be: hostility toward Jews as individuals, toward Judaism as a religion, toward the Jewish people as a group. Throughout history, it has expressed itself through religious prejudice, social exclusion, economic boycotts, restrictive laws, physical attacks, killings and exiling of identifiable Jews.

Different Types of Anti-Semitism

☐ Religious anti-Semitism: Through the Middle Ages, the persecution of the Jews was based on religious differences (rituals, belief in Jesus as the messiah, etc.). If Jews would convert to Christianity, they would be accepted. If they did not convert, they were segregated, expelled or killed.

☐ Secular anti-Semitism: Beginning around the 18th century, as Europe became less religious, Jews suffered social and economic discrimination. They were forced to live in restricted areas, denied citizenship, excluded from various occupations, etc. Even if they converted to Christianity, Christian communities would not accept them.

☐ Racial anti-Semitism: By the late 19th century, Jews were seen as an inferior and dangerous "race." Racists argued that, like blue eyes, historically determined cultural traits such as business skills were passed on through the genes. The "logic" of this thinking leads to extermination.

Summary: The history of anti-Semitism can, thus, be summed up as described by Raul Hilberg in *The Destruction of the European Jews* as

— Religious: You may not live among us as Jews.

— Secular: You may not live among us.

— Racial: You may not live.

POLITICS

Questions

1. What were some German reactions to the defeat in World War I?

2. What type of government did many German people prefer to the democratic Weimar Republic?

3. How did some politicians use anti-Semitism after World War I?

4. Compare the medieval view of the Jew as scapegoat to the view held by political leaders like Hitler in the 20th century.

In 1918, Germany lost World War I. With the Allies fast approaching, Kaiser Wilhelm fled, leaving Germany without an official representative to negotiate with the victors. The new government, the Weimar Republic, therefore, seemed to be a product of Germany's defeat.

The Weimar Republic was a federal republic (like the United States) composed of states such as Prussia and Bavaria. It had a democratic constitution, which allowed for a *Reichstag* (parliament), a president, a chancellor and a cabinet of ministers. The constitution guaranteed civil rights and basic freedoms. It provided for elections and a multiple party system. The new government's first official act, unfortunately, was the signing of the Versailles Treaty in 1919, which ended World War I. In this treaty, Germany was forced by Allied representatives to accept total defeat and total responsibility for starting the war. The Weimar Republic accepted defeat; a defeat the majority of Germans did not understand.

The German people were bewildered by the defeat. During the war, they had received news only through the severely censored government newspapers. No foreign soldier was on German soil when the German armies surrendered. Only the military and political leaders knew that they were utterly defeated and that the Allied forces (France, England, the U.S.) threatened to devastate Germany by starvation and armed force. These facts were not made public, even after the armistice (cease fire).

Many Germans felt there had been some betrayal behind the scenes. The Dolchstosslegende {*dolsh-shtoss-leggendeh*} or "stab in the back legend" became widely believed. Extremists linked Germany's defeat to false stories of Communist and Jewish conspiracies to dominate the world. Some famous Jews had participated actively in radical or revolutionary movements in Europe. For example, many were active in the Russian Communist Revolution of 1917.

The 1920s were a time of political crisis and turmoil in Germany. People of various political viewpoints were dissatisfied with the Weimar Republic because of its role in Germany's surrender. Some groups on the political right wanted to re-establish an old-style monarchy. Other groups on the political left wanted to establish a communistic people's government (called a Soviet). There were several attempts to overthrow the new government. Also, right-wing, armed gangs called *Freikorps,* who belonged to extreme nationalist groups like the National Socialist or Nazi Party, fought Communist demonstrators in the streets all over Germany.

Freikorps often attacked Jews and Jewish businesses. Perhaps the most infamous example of such assaults occurred in 1921. The German Foreign Minister, Walther Rathenau, was assassinated by a fanatical member of an ultra-nationalist group. Rathenau had been a staunch supporter of the Kaiser. He had organized the war economy and was responsible for Germany's remarkable ability to continue to fight until 1918. Devoted to Germany, he then became a central figure in the Weimar Republic. Rathenau was a Jew. Despite his patriotism, Rathenau was identified by anti-Semitic groups as a symbol of their invented "Jewish conspiracy" to dominate the world. Rathenau's murderers believed that no Jew should or could represent Germany. Although he was totally dedicated to his country, they killed him. His assassination robbed Germany of one of its ablest economic administrators who was internationally respected.

Opponents of the Weimar Republic were generally anti-Jewish. They accused Jews of being traitors, responsible for Communism and, at the same time, responsible for all that Communism opposed. In short, these groups blamed whatever seemed to be wrong with the country on the Jews. Facts simply were irrelevant; the Jews again became scapegoats.

Many Germans felt humiliated by the World War I defeat. They had lost national pride and had a negative national self-image. Millions were unemployed. Because of the startling changes brought about by the war and its aftermath—loss of the war, change of government, violence in the streets, inflation—many Germans felt a sense of alienation and confusion. They were drawn to political parties that wanted to regain lost territory, rearm and expand the army, return to an aggressive stand and oppose Communism at all costs. They looked for political parties with strong leaders. Those political parties talked of rejecting the Versailles Treaty, the new Republic and democratic institutions. Almost all such groups were anti-Semitic.

On November 9, 1923, Adolf Hitler and his young Nazi (or National Socialist) Party attempted to seize power in Munich, Bavaria. (Munich is the capital of Bavaria, the second-largest state in Germany.) The Nazis accused all their political opponents of treason, greed and conspiracy, which they said had brought about Germany's defeat in World War I.

Having attempted to overthrow the state government of Bavaria by force in the so-called Beer-hall Putsch, Hitler was sentenced to five years in a minimum security prison. He served less than nine months. His trial gave him the opportunity to gain publicity. During the trial, the judges allowed him to rant his political speeches day after day. The judges and the public seemed willing to listen to his ideas. This was a bad omen for the Weimar Republic.

LESSON 4

The Aftermath of World War I: Germans, Jews and Anti-Semitism

Reading 4A

INTERVIEWS WITH A GERMAN JEWISH FATHER FROM 1925-1945

Read each question first. Then, follow along as the text of the interview is read aloud in class. Finally, be prepared to discuss the questions.

Questions

1. Does the man in the interview see himself as German or Jewish?

2. What does the man mean when he says anti-Semitism in Germany is a "protest against poor economic conditions"?

3. Why does the man refuse to leave Germany in 1935?

4. Why do you think the man finds the events of 1935-1938 so unbelievable?

5. What is the significance of the story of the guard at Auschwitz?

(The following interview is based on actual interviews with three German Jewish victims of the Holocaust who survived. The father is a composite of the three.)

INTERVIEW WITH A GERMAN JEWISH FATHER, 1925

Q: Can you describe your family?

A: My family has lived in Berlin since 1795. My ancestors knew the great Moses Mendelssohn, the finest German Jew. My grandfather fought against the French in the Franco-Prussian War of 1871, and my father fought them in the Great War (World War I). He was decorated with the highest military honor, the Iron Cross. My older brother and uncle also fought in that war; my uncle lost a leg and my brother was blinded in a poison gas attack. Members of my family have been great German patriots devoted to the *Reich* for 125 years.

Q: What is your occupation?

A: I run the newspaper my father edited. My family and I supported Kaiser Wilhelm before the war through our newspaper, but now we feel we must give loyalty to the Weimar Republic. It stands for all that is best in Germany: freedom, tolerance, reason, justice and international peace.

Q: Do you belong to a synagogue?

A: Yes. But it is a matter of personal choice. My religious persuasion is not important. I am a good German—first, last and always. A very good German.

Q: Do you think there is anti-Semitism in Germany?

A: Yes, but it is unimportant and less than anywhere else. *True* Germans are not anti-Semitic. They believe in the values of their forefathers: tolerance, reason, equality, like Goethe, Lessing and Mendelssohn. Any German anti-Semitism is a protest against poor economic conditions. It will pass—this is an enlightened country, civilized and free. A land of laws and great traditions. We Germans are the most advanced, humanitarian people on earth.

SECOND INTERVIEW WITH A GERMAN JEWISH FATHER, NOVEMBER 1935

NOTE: Between April 1933 and November 1935, the Nazi government passed many anti-Jewish laws.

Q: With all the laws passed since 1933, how has life changed for you and your family?

A: Life under Hitler's government is more difficult for Jews. My children cannot attend the public school any more; my newspaper has been shut down; our non-Jewish friends don't see us much any more; we cannot fly the German flag; I have had to release our non-Jewish maid; and I am earning money sweeping floors.

Q: Do you think you will leave Germany?

A: No. This cannot last. Anti-Semitism has come before and gone away. Germans will not allow such discrimination for long. We are sometimes harassed on the streets by SA hoodlums, but there has been nothing like pogroms or mass violence. They are burning books, not authors. It will pass—how long can Hitler last?

THIRD INTERVIEW WITH A GERMAN JEWISH FATHER, SEPTEMBER 1938

Q: Because of the curfews and other restrictions, much more has changed in your life. For example, you are in new living quarters. Do you mind?

A: We have had to adapt and adjust to a new life. My family of four plus another family of four are living in two rooms. This has not been easy. We share a small bathroom and sleep on the floor. But we manage.

Q: What else has changed?

A: We have lost most of our savings because the government has seized Jewish bank accounts and property. Food is now rationed to us. We are forbidden to attend certain public places of entertainment; parks and public transportation are closed to us.

Q: Have you experienced any more harassment?

A: Yes. Sometimes on the streets one of us will be ridiculed, pushed or struck. The police are now under SS control, so they are usually no help. Yesterday, our neighbor was forced by some SA men to wear a sign saying he was a Jewish pig. When he went to the police, they forced him to wear a second sign saying he would never complain again.

Q: Have your attitudes about Germany changed?

A: Only about some Germans. This is unexplainable. Germany seems to have gone berserk. It is not the country I know as Germany. Violence has increased in the streets, book burnings occur regularly, people are arrested with no explanation and held indefinitely. I do not understand it. Concentration camps in the land of Goethe and Lessing? The land of Beethoven and Bach? My family does not understand. We still have hope—no one has been beaten or murdered in my family. We at least know clearly what is permitted and not permitted. They are burning books now; five hundred years ago they would have burned the authors.

FOURTH INTERVIEW WITH A GERMAN JEWISH FATHER, 1945

Q: The war is over. You are alone, that is, without your family, here in the Landsberg Displaced Persons (DP) Camp. How did you get here?

A: In January 1945 I was in Auschwitz. The Germans forced us onto the road and we ran, in the cold, for three days. I wound up at a camp called Mauthausen in Austria and from there was marched to Landsberg work camp. I was nearly dead: starving, with dysentery and lice, exhausted and even unable to get out of my bunk. I looked out the barracks window and saw a tank with a white star on it. The Americans had arrived.

Q: What did you think then?

A: No one thought any more. We were frightened or beyond fright. The Americans ordered us out. They couldn't believe their eyes—we looked like skeletons, emaciated, smelled of filth, disease, excrement and death. Some prisoners even had their flesh falling off their bones. The Americans made us strip—like the Germans had—and sprayed us with disinfectant. They fed us, gave us medical care and took down the barbed wire. Landsberg became a DP camp.

Q: Have you remained here since May?

A: No. I returned to Berlin to look for my family and then came back here.

Q: Are you alone?

A: No one is alive. In January 1942 Jews had to give up all warm clothing. My wife contracted pneumonia and died within a week. My son was taken away a few months later. He died in a slave labor camp in Poland. My brother was sent from Dachau to Auschwitz around the same time. Since he was nearly blind from his World War I experience with poison gas, he was sent immediately to the gas chamber when he arrived in Auschwitz. I believe the same gas that blinded him, or one like it, killed him at last. My uncle, who had lost a leg, was also sent to Auschwitz but died in the boxcar en route. I learned these things from people who survived Auschwitz. While we were still in Berlin, my daughter died in my arms of malnutrition in 1943, just before I was deported to Auschwitz. I had hoped my son had survived, or my brother—or someone. Now I don't know why I survived—what is left to live for?

Q: Are you angry?

A: Yes, angry—but at whom? I don't know. What good is anger, what good is life if it is lived alone?

Q: How do you feel about Germany and the Germans?

A: I don't know. A guard at Auschwitz used to discuss Goethe, the poet of humanity, and German philosophy with us. Then he would leave the discussion to "process" a train transport. That means he would go to send thousands of people to their deaths. Then he would return to our discussion. How could this be? They had gone beyond burning books and *did* burn the authors. Philosophy and mass murder? Art and medical experiments on human beings? Beethoven and gas chambers? Buchenwald concentration camp was built around the Goethe Oak where the poet used to sit and write! Germans are beasts—they are poets. How could they do it—make us so alone? I don't know . . .

LESSON 5

Hitler and the Nazi Party

HOLOCAUST CURRICULUM

HITLER

Hitler and the Nazi Party

TIMETABLE OF THE RISE OF NAZISM

Read all of Reading 5A, the "Timetable of the Rise of Nazism." Then, answer the questions on the Study Guide by referring to the "Timetable."

1. a. November 9, 1918: Weimar Republic declared.

   b. November 11, 1918: Armistice. Germany defeated in World War I.

2. June 28, 1919: Formal Treaty of Versailles is signed by representatives of the new Weimar government. Germany surrenders unconditionally.

3. a. July 1919: Hitler joins the DAP, *Deutsche Arbeiters Partei* (German Workers Party), a nationalistic, anti-Semitic, anti-democratic group in Munich.

   b. April 1920: Hitler gains leadership of the party and changes its name in order to draw voters from all sides. The new name is the National Socialist German Workers Party (NSDAP).

4. April 1920: Twenty-five point program of NSDAP is drafted. Three central ideas are:

   a. Jews are a genetic threat to all good, pure Germans and to all "Aryans."

   b. All members of the Party (and after 1933, all citizens of Germany) must adhere to the *Fuehrer* Principle, the idea of complete obedience to the will of the leader.

   c. Germans must have more *Lebensraum*, living space, to be taken from the "inferior slavic peoples in Eastern Europe (Russians, Poles, etc.)."

5. a. January 1923: French troops occupy the Ruhr Valley (German industrial region) because Germany falls behind in reparation payments to France. France demands that the coal mined by German workers from the Ruhr Valley be given to the French government as a substitute for the payments.

   b. German coal miners in the Ruhr Valley begin "passive resistance" by striking. They are joined by other German workers—barbers, grocers, doctors, police—who refuse to serve the French. The Weimar government approves of this. Coal mines shut down and the government pays wages to the workers and any losses the companies incur. Billions of German marks are spent.

6. a. April-November 1923: French troops anger German workers and citizens in the Ruhr Valley. Some Germans are upset at the lack of armed protest from the Weimar government.

   b. German workers, with the secret blessing of the government, derail French trains, blow up bridges, attack French soldiers. German ultra-nationalist feelings, combined with extreme anti-French feelings, become widespread.

   c. The results of the French occupation are disastrous: 152 civilians are killed. The enormous financial loss suffered by the Weimar government in the Ruhr Valley makes money meaningless. The German government pays out 3.5 billion marks; inflation reaches unbelievable heights; one administration after another is voted out of office. Because of the economic turmoil, as money loses its value, people's life savings evaporate.

7. 1921-23: Rampant inflation. By October 1923, a trillion marks to the dollar. Bread and butter cost trillions of marks. A bushel basket of money would not even buy a loaf of bread, and a wheel barrow of money bought a postage stamp.

8. November 9, 1923: Munich (Beer-hall) Putsch. Hitler attempts to seize the Bavarian government in Munich. He is tried for treason, sentenced to five years and serves fewer than nine months.

9. a. 1924-1925: Ruhr evacuated by French troops because of the Weimar government's negotiations with France. Currency is stabilized in Germany. German reparations are reduced by the Allies. American and British loans granted to Germany.

   b. As a result of the events of 1924-1925, Nazis do poorly in elections.

   c. Weimar government gains strength.

   d. In order to provide jobs for more people, the Weimar government begins to consider proposals to nationalize big industry and divide large estates. Thus, powerful industrialists and wealthy aristocratic estate owners begin to support Hitler who is opposed to the Weimar Republic.

10. October 1929: Depression. Unemployment rises. Foreign loans stop and are recalled.

11. September 1930: Elections. Nazis go from 800,000 votes in 1929 to 6.5 million votes and from 12 to 107 seats in the *Reichstag* (Parliament), about 25 percent of the total.

12. a. 1930-1932: Nazi hostility toward the "November Criminals," a Nazi term for the founders and supporters of the Weimar Republic, increases.

    b. Continuing to claim that Jews were the evil masterminds of the Weimar Republic, the Nazis increase their physical attacks on Jews and Jewish businesses.

13. October 1931: Nazis, army generals, industrialists, financiers and aristocrats all form the "National Front" against Communism. Because of this, the NSDAP gains more respectability and receives large contributions of money.

14. March 1932: Presidential elections. Hitler loses to Hindenburg but gets 13.5 million votes. In July, the NSDAP gets 230 seats in the *Reichstag,* 30 percent of the total.

15. January 30, 1933: Hitler is appointed chancellor of Germany by President Hindenburg.

16. March 23, 1933: The *Reichstag* approves the Enabling Act, which empowers Hitler to enact laws without the approval of the *Reichstag.*

17. July 14, 1933: The Nazi Party is proclaimed by law to be the one and only legal political party in Germany.

STUDY GUIDE QUESTIONS FOR THE "TIMETABLE OF THE RISE OF NAZISM"

Part I: Time Line. Place the letter of the event under the year it occurred.

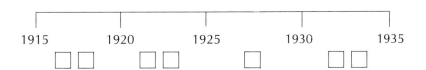

A. Hitler attempts to take control of a state government.

B. Cost of living soars in Germany.

C. Signing of the Versailles Treaty which ended World War I.

D. World-wide economic collapse.

E. Formation of the Weimar Republic.

F. President Hindenburg appoints Adolf Hitler chancellor.

G. Dramatic increase in Nazi support.

Part II: Matching and Short Answer

1. Match the characteristics of the DAP (German Workers Party) with the corresponding central ideas of the NSDAP (National Socialists German Workers Party).

DAP	NSDAP
_____ nationalistic	A. Jews are a genetic threat to all good, pure Germans and to all "Aryans."
_____ anti-Semitic	B. All members of the party must adhere to the *Fuehrer* Principle, the idea of complete obedience to the will of the leader.
_____ anti-democratic	C. Germans must have *Lebensraum*, living space, to be taken from the "inferior slavic peoples in Eastern Europe."

2. What does *Lebensraum* mean?

3. How did the Germans react to the French occupation of the Ruhr Valley?

4. Why did many wealthy Germans begin to support Hitler?

5. What did the term "November Criminals" mean?

6. What was the "National Front"?

7. What was the purpose of the Enabling Act of March 1933?

8. What happened on July 14, 1933, that determined the fate of German political opponents of the Nazis?

Part III

Based on your understanding of the Timetable, pick what you think are three key events that contributed most to the rise of Nazism. Support your point of view.

a.

b.

c.

BRIEF BIOGRAPHY OF ADOLF HITLER

Adolf Hitler was born in Linz, Austria. His mother seems to have been a kind woman. His strict father was an Austrian government worker. Hitler was almost constantly fighting with his father. Against his father's wishes, he went to Vienna as a young man to study art. He was refused entrance into an art school. Impoverished, he became one of Vienna's unemployed eking out a living painting post cards. Living in a flop-house, a cheap men's hotel, in Vienna, he began to listen to street corner anti-Semitic speakers. He later said he learned "the truth about the international Jew" in Vienna.

Hitler enlisted in the German army when World War I broke out and claimed, in his autobiographical *Mein Kampf* (My Struggle), that he was astonished to discover that Germany had lost the war in 1918. After World War I, unemployed again, he moved to Germany where he joined the newly-formed German Workers Party in 1920. After Hitler failed to seize the government of Bavaria, a state in Southern Germany, in 1923, it seemed as if his political career was over. Nevertheless, turning to legal methods of gaining political power, Hitler worked behind the scenes to rebuild his party. In the 1925 presidential elections, Hitler convinced the World War I commanding general, Erich von Ludendorff, to run on the Nazi ticket. The Nazis failed miserably as Hindenburg was elected with an overwhelming majority. In 1932, Hitler himself ran for president. Although he was defeated by Hindenburg, Hitler received over 36 percent of the popular vote, more than thirteen million votes.

For many reasons, Hitler's support had grown between 1925 and 1932. He was among the first to employ modern techniques for election campaigns. His use of fast cars and airplanes allowed him to speak to thousands of people each day. His professional propagandists and film makers used radio and film to create an image of *Der Fuehrer*, The Leader, as confident, strong and concerned. He was unmatched as a public speaker and took great pride in his ability to manipulate and intimidate people. In the end, it was not what Hitler said to crowds of thousands that mattered but how he said it. Slogans and carefully staged meetings and rallies gave the country the impression that he could do no wrong and knew exactly what Germany needed.

In 1933, President von Hindenburg and his political advisors perceived Hitler as an uneducated gutter politician. Yet, they believed that only Hitler could bring a stop to the violence in the streets often caused by Nazi Brown Shirts (SA men). Convinced that he would be able to control Hitler, Hindenburg appointed him chancellor on January 30, 1933. Hitler was 44 years old.

By March 1933, it was clear that Hindenburg had been seriously mistaken about controlling Hitler. The chancellor used a variety of methods to gain total power and govern Germany as a dictator. He manipulated the mass media. He invented a Communist conspiracy which he claimed was directed at dominating Germany. In order to save the country from this Communist threat, he said, the civil rights guaranteed by the Weimar Constitution had to be eliminated. Even Hindenburg seemed to believe in the conspiracy theory.

The President allowed Hitler to replace the constitution with a series of emergency decrees. One of the most sweeping was the Enabling Act. This act gave Hitler the right to govern Germany by passing laws without approval of the *Reichstag* (parliament). Based on such emergency decrees, he shut down newspapers, radio stations, trade unions and opposition political parties. He also had government agencies write laws that began to remove Jews from German society and from the economy.

Under Hitler's rule, Germany seemed to be regaining prestige. In accordance with the Versailles Treaty, some of the territory lost after World War I was returned to Germany. Hitler strengthened the army in spite of the Versailles Treaty which had limited the German armed forces. Arms industries helped pull Germany out of the depression, and unemployment was reduced drastically. Other countries seemed to support Hitler whom they saw as a defense against Communism and the Soviet Union. It seemed that his promise of "law and order" was being kept. The police were everywhere, and it was safe for most Germans to walk the streets at night.

All those thought to hold anti-Nazi opinions, however, or Jews or those suspected of not supporting the Nazi government were subject to arrest and/or beatings. People were taken from their homes or off the streets to the newly opened concentration camps. They might be kept there for years without any news of their whereabouts being sent to their families. Upon release, they were made to swear they would remain silent about their experiences in the camp under the threat of being rearrested along with their families. Few were willing to break that promise knowing their families might be endangered.

Hitler believed that to maintain power his philosophy had to be aimed at Germany's young people. In December 1936, he passed the "Law Concerning the Hitler Youth." Under that law, all young people in Germany had to join the Hitler Youth. Article 2 of the law stated that "the entire German youth is to be educated physically, mentally and morally in the Hitler Youth in the spirit of National Socialism." Young people now owed their allegiance first and foremost to their Fuehrer, Hitler, even if it meant abandoning their families, traditions, religion and friends. Germany would be "united in its youth."

By 1938, Hitler boasted that Germany would become an empire that would rule Europe for 1000 years. At first, his success was astonishing. For example, with no resistance, German-speaking Austria became part of the Third Reich, Hitler's "Third Empire," in 1938. A half-million Austrians greeted their new leader with joyous cries of " Heil Hitler!" as he rode triumphantly through the streets of Vienna.

Obsessed with obtaining *Lebensraum* (living space), Hitler led Germany into World War II and destruction. Because of his fanatical desire to create an "Aryan" Europe for Germans, he ordered what one historian has called "the war against the Jews," the attempted genocide of all Europe's Jews. World War II was to gain space for the Germans; the war against the Jews was to guarantee "purity of race." These were two wars. They were related because they happened on the same territory at the same time, but they were two separate issues in Hitler's mind.

Hitler was a powerful, clever and ruthless politician. He totally dominated Germany and then most of Europe during World War II. Hitler promised the German people glory and prosperity. His promises were offered in empty slogans and phrases that masked lies or irrational arguments. Yet, because of his magnetic style, many people accepted those slogans and phrases without thinking. Hitler could not have caused the Holocaust or World War II by himself, but neither of those events could have occurred without him. By 1945, he was responsible for the death of nearly 6 million Jews and an estimated 40 million more men, women and children.

Hitler committed suicide in May 1945, as the Soviet Army approached his underground bunker in Berlin.

L E S S O N 6

Hitler and the Nazi Party

Reading 6A

Question

Choose two beliefs of the Nazi Party. Why might these beliefs have appealed to some Germans?

THE BELIEFS OF THE NAZI PARTY

The National Socialist German Workers Party (known as the Nazi Party) was the most nationalistic of the many German political parties of the Weimar Republic. The handbook of the party began with the fundamental rule of the *Fuehrer* or Leader Principle. This stated that all power was "in the leader *(Fuehrer)*" who had to be obeyed at all costs.

The core of the Nazi Party ideology, its collection of ideas and beliefs, was exclusion. According to the Nazis, all those who were not "of pure Aryan blood" were excluded from the party and even from German citizenship. This policy was based on the racist philosophy known as Aryanism. The word "Aryan" or "Nordic" was applied to those who were white-skinned, light-haired and light-eyed. Nazi scientists established other criteria for Aryan status: skull size, height, ancestral religion, energy and strength. These people were said to be "pure" descendants of the ancient Greeks and Romans. "Pure" meant that they had not bred outside their own race.

The Aryans' most important characteristic was a shared "race-soul." Quiet, strong, innocent and good, their mission was to defeat evil. In this fantasy, the bearers of evil in the world had been and continued to be the Jews, referred to as a "race." Jews epitomized mixing of races and, therefore, weakening of the "blood." As a "weak race," they were the bearers of disease and would ultimately destroy the healthy and innocent Aryan race-soul.

Aryanism insisted that all racial characteristics were determined internally, by the soul and the "blood," and not by environment or culture. Therefore, Jews would remain Jews no matter how long they had lived with Germans and no matter what religion they or their ancestors had adopted. Aryans, as long as they avoided marrying Jews, would remain Aryans no matter what.

In a pure Aryan state, Jews would be treated as foreigners and would not have the right to vote. All their civil rights under German law would also be removed from them. Thus, Jews would not be able to count on police protection. They would not be able to appeal to the law courts for any injustice done to them. They would not have the right to attend schools or participate as equals in any part of society.

The Nazis insisted that the Versailles Treaty must be rejected and all reparations ended. They believed that Germany must once again take a position as a strong and forceful power in the world. One of Germany's main missions would be to fight communism.

According to the Nazi views, Germans must learn again what it meant to be a "good" German: obedience to authority and unquestioning devotion to traditional German values. All Germans should be reeducated: women should be in the home raising children; men should cultivate the "manly virtues" as soldiers or workers for the Fatherland. Nazi leaders claimed the modern world was too permissive. It was filled with corrupt politics, pornography, sensual art and literature and sexual promiscuity. Such modern things were to be combatted.

Hitler offered the Nazi ideology to mass audiences. He skillfully combined notions of German nationalism with fears of foreign, communist or "racial" corruption. He presented the myth of the "Aryan race," and he defined its members as *Uebermenschen* or "overmen" or "supermen." This super-race, according to Hitler, was destined to dominate the world because of its purity and strength. He believed the world was governed by a kind of jungle law. In such a world, the strongest and purest would naturally triumph.

According to Hitler, the danger to the "Aryan race" came from its opposite, the "Jewish race." He believed that by mixing and polluting the blood of the "Aryans," Jews had "infiltrated" German culture, politics and thinking. The Jews, he said, had been the underlying cause of the German defeat in World War I. They were responsible for Germany's loss of territory or *Lebensraum* or "living space."

It followed from his racial theories of life that in order to save the "Aryan race" and ultimately the world, "inferior races" like the Jews had to be first isolated and then eliminated. The beliefs of the Nazi Party became the policies of the Nazi state.

Reading 6B

THE *FUEHRER* SPEAKS

CAST

An American Reporter, Narrator, Hitler Youth Member, Hitler, Five Members of the Audience, Edward R. Murrow, Ernie Pyle, William Shirer.

(WAGNERIAN MUSIC IS PLAYING IN THE BACKGROUND)

AMERICAN REPORTER STANDING OFF TO ONE SIDE SPEAKING CLOSELY INTO MICROPHONE: Here we are at a Nazi rally. Thirty thousand people are packed into a huge hall. Brightly colored flags are draped from the ceilings and walls. A band is playing military music. Many people in the crowd have on different types of uniforms—Hitler Youth, the SA, the SS and others. Hitler's arrival is always dramatic. The band stops and a hush falls over the enormous crowd. Then, at the moment he enters from the back of the hall, the band begins to play a triumphal march. The *Fuehrer* strides down the aisle slowly as thirty thousand hands go up in salute.

NARRATOR: By observing a Nazi rally, we can begin to understand some of the reasons for Hitler's success. The rituals of this rally are always practiced. They had been carefully developed from the early days. "In such an atmosphere," said one American reporter, "no wonder that every word dropped by Hitler seemed like an inspired Word from on high." In the middle of the crowds, our roving reporter stops to interview an enthusiastic teenager in a Hitler Youth uniform.

REPORTER: Do you remember the first time you saw the *Fuehrer?*

HITLER YOUTH MEMBER: "Of course! I was six years old. On that March evening, perched on the shoulders of my Uncle Franz, I watched a torchlight parade of brown-shirted storm troopers and Hitler Youth formations, through a flag-draped marketplace packed with what seemed to be the whole population. Clusters of people hung from windows and balconies, and a continuous storm of 'Heil Hitler!' drowned out the music of the . . . military band. But what drove the populace into a fever pitch of excitement was the man who stood in a black, open Mercedes . . . in front of the medieval city hall. He acknowledged the near-delirious homage of the crowd. I will never forget the rapture he invoked that night. On that evening, Hitler surely symbolized the promise of a new Germany, a proud *Reich* that had once again found its rightful place . . ."

NARRATOR: The youth stops talking as Hitler begins to speak.

(AUDIENCE MEMBERS SHOULD CHEER WHERE INDICATED)

HITLER: Stands straight at podium, with head high, looking almost into the distance. Places both fists against chest as he speaks of ''we.''

We and we alone stand for the rebirth of Germany.

(Points fist straight ahead with each phrase.)

One Empire! One People! One Leader!

(AUDIENCE CHEERS)

We will struggle for the victory of the Aryan race and its soul of purity and strength!

(Lowers voice, leans forward and shakes head slowly—almost whispers.)

The politics of democracy has divided Germany against itself, made Germans materialistic, turned them from their roots in the soil and from their holy racial qualities that come from the blood and the land.

(Raises voice gradually and straightens up.)

No longer will there be political parties! No longer will society be subjected to the whims of the evil forces that have seeped into the body of the people, of the nation.

(Strikes chest with right fist upon speaking the words ''We alone'' then keeps hand at his chest.)

We alone will be able to carry out the necessary social reforms to cure our nation of its diseases.

(AUDIENCE CHEERS)

(Lowers voice, dramatically.)

The infection and pollution of international finance has weakened Germany. We will cure it. We will make it strong again, as it was meant to be and as it was long ago. If we wish to carry out these social reforms, then the struggle must go hand in hand against the opponents of every social arrangement:

(Dramatic pause, then almost growls the next two words.)

the Jews.

(Slowly shakes head ''no'' throughout next sentence.)

Here, too, we know exactly that just scientific, intellectual understanding is not enough.

(Deliberate, emphasizing each word.)

After understanding must come organization, which changes into—

(Brief pause, looks at the audience, stares at one person and almost whispers next word.)

Action.

(AUDIENCE CHEERS AND CONTINUES CHEERING AS HE SPEAKS)

(Raises voice, almost yelling.)

Action is our cry!

(AUDIENCE CHEERS AND STOPS)

And the deed, the action remains firm:

(Pause. Emphasizes each of the underlined words by striking the table or podium with fist on each word.)

removal of the Jews from our nation!

(AUDIENCE CHEERS)

(Quieter in normal tones, but still loud.)

Not because we would begrudge them their existence—we congratulate the rest of the world on their company—but because the existence of our own nation is a thousand times more important to us than that of an alien race.

(Leans forward shaking head "no.")

There can be no compromises! There are only two possibilities—either victory of the Aryan or annihilation of the Aryan and victory of the Jew.

(Speaks with disgust, drawing out the word "vermin" and making it sound the same as the word "Bolsheviks.")

Like vermin the Bolsheviks have infiltrated our people.

(Continues to speak slowly, as if to make an important point.)

The Jewish-Bolshevik conspiracy has advanced almost to victory.

(Pauses, looks around and then speaks the next two words evenly and almost quietly.)

Until now.

(Looks to heaven and puts fists to chest; almost sobs the first two words.)

We alone will know how to eradicate the threat. We will defeat it once and for all.

(AUDIENCE CHEERS)

(Spreads arms and looks out at the audience.)

We know the solution to the Jewish problem in Germany.

(Points finger straight ahead and glowers.)

If at the beginning of the War of 1914 to 1918 and during the War, twelve or fifteen thousand of these Hebrew corrupters of the people had been held under the poison gas, as happened to hundreds of thousands of our very best German workers in the field, the sacrifice of millions at the front would not have been in vain.

(Continues, getting louder and faster but pausing after each phrase, gesturing with his hands at each phrase.)

These race-polluters, defilers of the blood, these perverted enemies of the Aryan race have defiled our blood and society. They have crawled into every place in the culture: science, art, newspapers, business, banking, politics, everywhere!

(Quick horizontal motion of both hands across body like umpire's safe sign.)

Jewish-Bolshevik art will be banned.

(Gestures with hands as if breaking something in half. Voice gets louder gradually.)

Jewish businesses and newspapers and banks will be destroyed. Jewish-Bolshevik politics will be exterminated. And, even if German science must come to a halt for a hundred years, Jewish science will be removed. They will be cut out root and branch from our midst.

(AUDIENCE CHEERS)

(Looks to heaven again, raising both hands and exclaiming.)

Germany will be clean of Jews! And the Aryan will prosper, will multiply, will inherit his true place throughout Europe—

(Yells, emphasizing each word with voice and raising right hand, outstretched straight up for each two word phrase.)

ONE EMPIRE! ONE PEOPLE! ONE LEADER!

(Louder still.)

SIEG—HEIL! FOR VICTORY—HAIL!

(AUDIENCE CHEERS)

(Hitler continues to yell with both fists shaking stretched out in front of him as if punching the air.)

If we must go to war again for our rightful place as the most powerful and heroic Aryan people, then the Jews will pay dearly for their crimes of November 1918! If there will be war, then the Jews of Europe will be destroyed. ONE EMPIRE! ONE PEOPLE! ONE LEADER! SIEG—HEIL!

(AUDIENCE CHEERS)

NARRATOR: Now we are in the International Broadcasting System's European studio in Munich, Germany. Present are three American reporters, Edward R. Murrow, William Shirer and Ernie Pyle. They are sitting around a table discussing Hitler's speech.

WILLIAM SHIRER: This was another rabble-rousing, stirring speech. But do you think the audience, those who listened over the radio as well as those who were there, listened thoughtfully? I had several questions.

EDWARD R. MURROW: You could feel the electricity in the air, all right. But what did some of those words and phrases mean? What, for example, did he mean by the "rebirth of Germany"? Was he implying that the country had died? Was that a symbolic reference to the German defeat in 1918? Or did he mean Germany was starting over? Has he written off the Weimar Republic altogether? His references to the end of democratic political parties seem very threatening.

ERNIE PYLE: More than that, what does "one empire" mean? Is Germany going to try to become a European empire again? Does "one people" mean that all the differences between the Germans are going to be removed? And "one leader" seems to imply a dictatorship that will remove any possibility of other German leaders directing the policies of the country.

SHIRER: He seemed to say that the "one people" would be the "Aryan" people. Does anybody know who they are? Is that a racial group? Is it a national group or an ethnic group? Who is going to decide who is "Aryan" and who isn't? These are all important questions. But the main question is: How many of those 30,000 people really listened to what Hitler said? Could all those people tolerate such horrible things said about the Jews?

MURROW: It seems clear that the Jews don't fit into Hitler's category of "Aryan" or German for that matter. That reference to poison gas in the First World War was not only gruesome, it was puzzling. Doesn't he know that among the tombstones of the German soldiers who died for Germany are 12,000 with Stars of David on them? This point was unclear to me—how could he attack German Jews, most of whom are strong German patriots?

PYLE: I would guess that few if any of the crowd cared about how many German Jews gave their lives for their country. In that electric atmosphere, not many people would think so clearly. It was frightening to see 30,000 hands go up and hear all those voices screaming "Sieg, Heil" together.

SHIRER: Perhaps this was another example of his use of rhetoric, speaking style, to cover up a lack of real meaning. Do you think those 30,000 people stopped to think about what any sentence meant?

MURROW: It was fascinating and frightening to see the crowd react with the salute and the shouting. There was little if any thoughtful response to what Hitler said. The crowd reacted to how he said it.

PYLE: What was most frightening was the talk of "Aryan purity." Does anyone know what that is? Surely some of those people in the audience were aware that talk of "pollution" of blood and race is preposterous.

SHIRER: Incidentally, how many Jewish banks and businesses are there in Germany? I believe that no banks are owned by Jews. And very few of the leading businesses and industries are owned by Jews. Yet, Hitler claims the Jews run the banks and the businesses. Is he deliberately lying?

PYLE: And how can he claim the Jews are all Bolsheviks? The Bolsheviks are anti-capitalist, that is, they want to destroy all banks and major private industries and businesses. It seems that Hitler accuses Jews of being with whatever group he is against.

MURROW: Will any of his people respond thoughtfully? Will he be tested in the public arena by our German counter-parts in the press and the media? Can anyone ask for definitions of his terms? Can we find out what his words really meant? In a democracy, it is every citizen's duty to think about what their leaders tell them and evaluate it rationally, not emotionally. Hitler's style and rhetoric prevent people from thinking about what he says.

PYLE: There seems to me no question that the Jews of Germany are in some danger. They may be expelled or lose their homes and possessions, as well as their civil rights. But when that happens, all Germans are in danger. Where will it stop once that first group is taken away? Germans, if it's not too late, need to carefully examine what this man tells them and asks them to tolerate. It is the fate of Germany, as well as of the Jews, that is at issue.

MURROW: Can we find any trace of critical thinking in a crowd? As Mr. Shirer here once wrote: "MAN'S—OR AT LEAST THE GERMAN'S—CRITICAL FACULTY IS SWEPT AWAY AT SUCH MOMENTS, AND EVERY LIE IS ACCEPTED AS HIGH TRUTH ITSELF."

L E S S O N 7

Toward the "Final Solution"

HOLOCAUST CURRICULUM

SOLUTION

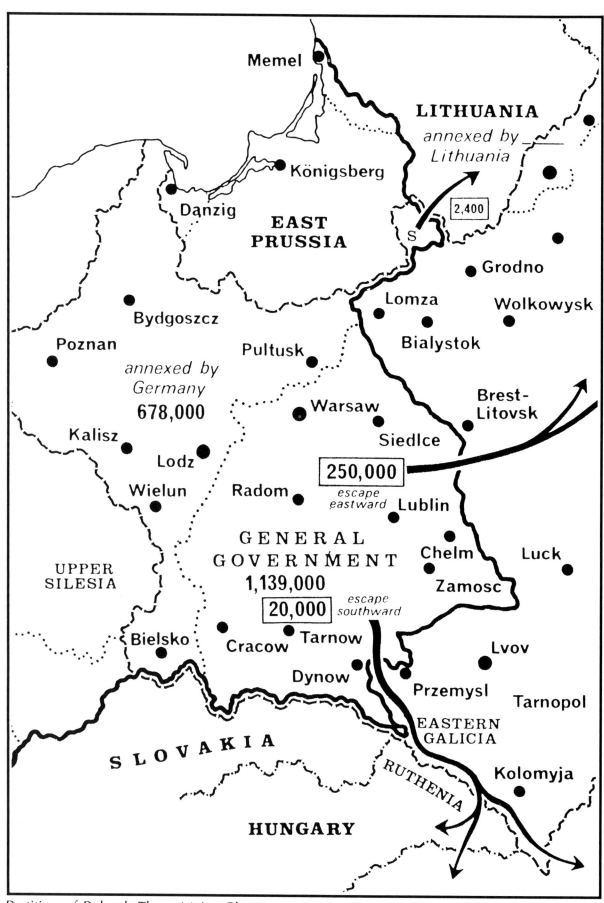

Memel

LITHUANIA
annexed by Lithuania

Königsberg

Danzig

EAST PRUSSIA

2,400

S

Grodno

Lomza

Wolkowysk

Bydgoszcz

Bialystok

Poznan

Pultusk

annexed by Germany
678,000

Warsaw

Brest-Litovsk

Siedlce

Kalisz

250,000

Lodz

escape eastward

Wielun

Radom

Lublin

GENERAL GOVERNMENT
1,139,000

Chelm

Luck

UPPER SILESIA

20,000

Zamosc

escape southward

Bielsko

Cracow

Tarnow

Lvov

Dynow

Przemysl

Tarnopol

EASTERN GALICIA

S L O V A K I A

RUTHENIA

Kolomyja

HUNGARY

Partition of Poland, Three Major Ghettos

OUTLINE: TOWARD THE "FINAL SOLUTION"

I. **Removal of the Jews from German Society:**

    A. **The First Solution:**

    B. **The Second Solution:**

    C. **The "Final Solution":**

        1. **1939:**

        2. **1941:**

II. **Preparatory Stages for the "Final Solution":**

    A. **Legislation:**

        1. **February 28, 1933; Emergency Decree for the "Protection of People and State":**

        2. **March 23, 1933; The Enabling Act, "Law for the Relieving of the Distress of People and *Reich*":**

        3. **April 1933; "Law for the Restoration of a Professional Civil Service":**

        4. **April 1933; "Law Regarding the Admission to the Bar":**

        5. **April 1933; "Law Against the Overcrowding of German Schools and Institutions of Higher Learning":**

6. July 14, 1933:

7. September 1935; *"Reich* Citizenship Law" and the "Law for the Protection of German Blood and Honor" (Nuremberg Laws):

   a.

   b.

   c.

      1)

      2)

      3)

      4)

B. **Consequences of the Laws:**

  1. **Concentration Camps Open:**

     a.

     b.

       1)

       2)

  2. **Removal of Jews:**

     a.

     b.

c.

d.

C. **Expulsion, Violence and Reaction:**

1. **Deportations:**

   a.

   b.

      1)

      2)

      3)

2. **The *Kristallnacht* (Night of the Broken Glass):**

   a.

   b.

      1)

      2)

      3)

c.

    1)

    2)

    3)

3. **General Reaction Was Quick:**

    a.

    b.

    c.

    d.

    e.

4. **Nazi Reaction:**

    a.

        1)

        2)

            a)

            b)

3)

4)

b.

1)

2)

D. **Development of Ghettos:**

1. **World War II Begins:**

2. **Defeat:**

a.

b.

3. **Ghettos:**

a.

b.

c.

d.

1)

    a)

    b)

2)

3)

4)

    a)

    b)

e.

f.

g.

h.

i.

j.

k.

l.

4. **Escape:**

    a. **Sanctity of the Family:**

    b. **Collective Responsibility:**

E. **Summary:**

    1. **First Stage:**

    2. **Second Stage:**

    3. **Third Stage:**

L E S S O N 8

Toward the "Final Solution"

There are no Readings in Lesson 8. Students will view the videotape "The *Kristallnacht* and Ghettos." A discussion will follow.

The "Final Solution" and its Perpetrators

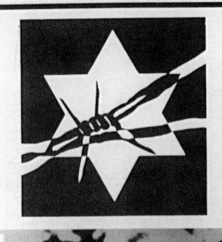

HOLOCAUST CURRICULUM

FINALS

The "Final Solution" and
its Perpetrators

The Death Camps

OUTLINE: THE "FINAL SOLUTION"

III. **The "Final Solution" to the "Jewish Problem":**

The "Final Solution" was the annihilation of the Jews. It began to take form with the invasion of Poland in 1939 and the institution of ghettos in 1940. Its last stage began in June 1941, when Germany broke the Nazi-Soviet Pact and invaded the Soviet Union, establishing six death camps in Poland (see map, p. 76).

A. **Inefficient Methods:**

1. *Einsatzgruppen:*

   a. **Responsibility:**

   b. **Secret Directive:**

      1) **Executive Measures:**

      2) **Code:**

   c. **Tasks:**

      1) **Gas Vans:**

         a)

         b)

2) **Mass Shootings:** *Einsatzgruppen* rounded up Jews, made them dig mass graves and shot them so they would fall into the graves they had dug.

a)

b)

c)

2. **Results of the Secret Directive and the *Einsatzgruppen*:**

B. **Efficient Methods:**

1. **The Decisive Order:** Just after the invasion of the Soviet Union, Hitler ordered the "Final Solution to the Jewish Question."

a. **Text:**

"I hereby charge you with making all necessary preparations with regard to organizational and financial matters for bringing about a complete solution to the Jewish question in the German sphere of influence in Europe. Wherever other government agencies are involved, they are to cooperate with you."

b. **Importance:** This was a turning point in history. All government agencies, all military forces, all the branches of the state were to participate in the pursuit of the annihilation of a specific group.

2. **The Perpetrators:**

   a. **Bureaucrats:**

      1)

      2)

         a)

         b)

         c)

         d)

         e)

The aim of the efficiency experts and bureaucrats was to get the victims to the killers as quickly as possible and with the least number of difficulties.

   b. **Creation of Death Camps:** In 1942, the construction of six death camps in Poland began. The main purpose of these camps would be the killing of Europe's Jews. The camps were located at Chelmno, Treblinka, Maidanek, Sobibor, Belzec and Auschwitz (see map, p. 76).

      1)

      2)

c. **Steps toward Extermination:**

   1) **Registration:**

   2) **Deportation:**

      a)

      b)

      c)

No Jews knew about the death camps. In 1942, many Germans were also unaware of the program of murder the bureaucrats had devised.

d. **Railroads:**

   1) **Scheduling:**

      a)

.

b)

    (1)

    (2)

    (3)

c)

2) **Cost:**

a)

b)

    (1)

    (2)

       (a) The SS was given excursion or group rates by the official state travel agency (the MITTEL-EUROPAEISCHE REISEBUERO or Middle-Europe Travel Bureau), which continued to handle tourist groups going to beaches in France or Greece while sending Jews to gas chambers in Poland.

(b) All such "special trains"—the vacation trains as well as the death ones—received excursion rates and were directed by the same bureaucrats. Children under ten, on vacation trains or death trains, rode for half-fare and children under four rode for free.

Deception was maintained at every step. The "Final Solution" was to be kept a state secret. Those among the German bureaucracy and SS who knew about the death camps were sworn to secrecy upon penalty of death. Yet, eventually, news of the train transports and of their destinations became known. While few people knew of the details of life in Auschwitz, many knew that the camps were places where Jews were mistreated, poorly fed, worked to exhaustion and killed. The scope of the atrocities and death, however, was not even imagined—not by Jews, Poles or most Germans.

3) **Business as Usual:** Almost all the railroad workers were aware of the "cargo" and destinations of the death trains. Yet, each focused *solely* on the narrow task of his job.

   a)

   b)

   c)

   d)

Millions of law-abiding citizens, concerned with their careers and the lives of their families, continued their routine jobs. Many of those jobs and those citizens were now in the service of the destruction process, the murder of the Jews of Europe. Business as usual made the Holocaust possible.

Reading 9B

BACKGROUND TO AUSCHWITZ

First, read the questions that precede the essay "Background to Auschwitz." Then, read the essay. Finally, answer the questions on a separate sheet of paper. The assignment should be handed in the following day.

Questions

1. Why was Auschwitz chosen as a site for a concentration camp?

2. How many camps were at Auschwitz, and how did they differ from each other?

3. Why were doctors important at the arrival of the trains at Auschwitz?

4. What was Zyklon B?

5. Approximately how many Jews were killed at Auschwitz?

6. Why were Jews and Gypsies murdered at Auschwitz?

BACKGROUND TO AUSCHWITZ

The small town of Oswiecem {os-svee-chem}, called Auschwitz in German, was located in Upper Silesia, Poland. During World War I, stables were converted into Polish army barracks just outside the town. Late in 1940, the Reichsfuehrer SS, Heinrich Himmler, decided to make use of the already constructed army barracks and selected Auschwitz to serve as a concentration camp—a place to concentrate "enemies of the Reich." From a relatively small area located on a swamp, Auschwitz would be expanded to 440 acres, housing close to 200,000 prisoners. It is unlikely that even Himmler foresaw this in 1940. In March 1941, Himmler told Rudolf Hoess, Commandant of Auschwitz, that Auschwitz had been selected as the main operations center for the murder of Europe's Jews.

Auschwitz was divided into three camps. Each camp housed thousands of prisoners, and each camp had a different function. Auschwitz I remained a concentration camp, housing political prisoners and "criminals" as defined by the German authorities. Auschwitz II-Birkenau was constructed between the end of 1941 and the middle of 1942 and became the death camp. Auschwitz III-Monowitz, where slave laborers were constructing what was to be the largest synthetic rubber factory in the world, was the I.G. Farben Buna plant. (I.G. Farben was the largest chemical-industrial conglomerate in the world. Buna was the name given to the synthetic rubber that was to be produced to make Germany self-sufficient in the war.) Auschwitz also included some 35 smaller labor camps within a 50-mile radius.

Trains arrived regularly at Auschwitz-Birkenau carrying cattle cars crammed with Jews from all parts of Europe. The Jews were driven off the trains onto a long railroad platform, and forced to line up and move toward the end of the platform where several SS men, directed by doctors, would determine who seemed capable of working and who would be "non-productive." At this selection process, these men sent people directly to their deaths with a flick of the thumb or wrist or a nod of the head. The "non-productive" category automatically included children under age 16 and adults over age 40, cripples, the mentally deficient, those already emaciated from starvation, mothers carrying small children and others deemed "non-productive" for no apparent reason.

Those who survived the selection were forced to do slave labor at Auschwitz III-Monowitz or at one of the smaller labor camps. Some were selected for the *Sonderkommando* (special duty). They were used to clear gas chambers of dead bodies and carry them to the crematoria to be burned. Most of these men were killed after three months when they were replaced by new prisoners. Other prisoners were given jobs in the camp such as kitchen or latrine duty. Those needed by the SS, such as carpenters or physicians, also were spared for a time. All prisoners were underfed and lived under miserable conditions. The SS doctors had calculated the number of calories given to prisoners. They rationed food so that no prisoner would survive more than three months. This led to savage behavior—stealing from other prisoners and secretly trying to steal from garbage heaps—surviving by any means.

The first experiments with a prussic acid gas called Zyklon B, previously used as insecticide, took place in September 1941. Before long, at Auschwitz-Birkenau, there were four enormous gas chambers, which could be used to murder 15,000 people daily. Their attached crematoria were used for disposing of the bodies. By the end of 1944, when Auschwitz was abandoned to the oncoming Russian armies, over 2½ million Jews had died of disease or starvation, or had been worked to death, gassed, shot, hung, injected with lethal drugs or experimentally tortured. Over 30,000 non-Jewish Polish prisoners were also murdered at Auschwitz, along with thousands of other political or national enemies of Germany. More than 250,000 Gypsies also were killed there. Jews and Gypsies were to be annihilated simply because they existed.

Reading 9C

Directions:

On the Daily Log of Activities, list every activity of one day, such as waking, washing, going to the bathroom, eating, working, studying, watching television, etc.

Daily Log of Activities

Name: _____

Date: _____

Activity

7:00 _____

8:00 _____

9:00 _____

10:00 _____

11:00 _____

12:00 _____

1:00 _____

2:00 _____

3:00 _____

4:00 _____

5:00 _____

6:00 _____

7:00 _____

8:00 _____

9:00 _____

10:00 _____

11:00 _____

12:00 _____

On the Calorie Tally list each item of food you eat during one day and add up the total number of calories.

Calorie Tally

	Food	**Calories**

Breakfast: _____   _____
    _____   _____
    _____   _____
    _____   _____
    _____   _____
    _____   _____
    _____   _____

Calorie Total: _____

Lunch: _____   _____
    _____   _____
    _____   _____
    _____   _____
    _____   _____
    _____   _____
    _____   _____

Calorie Total: _____

Dinner: _____   _____
    _____   _____
    _____   _____
    _____   _____
    _____   _____
    _____   _____
    _____   _____

Calorie Total: _____

Snacks: _____   _____
    _____   _____
    _____   _____
    _____   _____
    _____   _____
    _____   _____
    _____   _____

Calorie Total: _____

Total Calories for the Day: _____

Reading 9D

CALORIE TALLY

Food	Calories
Apple	70
Apple juice	125
Apple pie	373
Apple sauce (sweetened)	100
Apple sauce (unsweetened)	50
Asparagus	20
Bacon (2 slices)	98
Bagel	125
Banana	64
Banana cream pie	300
Beans (baked)	160
Beans (green)	14
Beans (lima)	100
Beef (4 oz)	450
Beef (ground, hamburger)	550
Beef (sirloin)	400
Beef (ribs)	600
Beef (steak)	400
Beef (corned)	300
Beets	45
Blintzes (2)	300
Blueberries (1/2 C)	90
Bologna (4 oz)	300
Bread (1 slice)	60
Bread (with margarine)	100
Butter(1 T)	100
Cabbage (1 C)	15
Cake	200
Candy	125
Cantaloupe	55
Carrots (1 raw)	20
Cereal (1 C)	100
Cheese (1 oz)	100
Cottage cheese (1C)	240
Cherries (1 C)	80
Chicken (broiled, 6 oz)	230
Chicken (fried)	300
Coffee	2
Cookies (1, avg. assortment)	50
Corn	70
Crackers (1, avg. assortment)	15
Doughnuts (1, avg. assortment)	165
Duck (6 oz)	500
Eggs (1 fried or scrambled)	110
Fish cakes (2)	300
Fish sticks (6)	250
Fruit salad	200
Gelatin	260
Grapefruit	·60

Grapes (1 C)	95
Gum	0
Ham (6 oz)	500
Honey (1 T)	65
Hot dog	150
Ice cream	150
Jam (1 T)	55
Knockwurst (6 oz)	500
Lamb (6 oz)	600
Lemonade	100
Liver (6 oz)	400
Liverwurst	300
Lobster	315
Macaroni (1/2 cup, boiled)	95
Margarine (1 T)	75
Mayonnaise (1 T)	110
Meat loaf (2 slices)	500
Milk (8 oz)	160
Nuts (1/4 C)	650
Onion rings	145
Oranges	65
Orange juice	115
Pancakes (1)	55
Pastry (avg.)	250
Peaches	35
Peanut butter (1 T)	95
Pears	100
Peas (1/2 C)	70
Pickles	15
Pie (avg.)	325
Pizza (1 slice)	250
Popcorn (1 C)	55
Pork chop (4 oz)	300
Potato chips (10)	115
Potatoes (avg.)	100
Raisins (1/4 C)	115
Rice (1 C)	185
Rolls	160
Salad	50
Salad dressing (1 T)	105
Salami (4 oz)	350
Sausage (4 oz)	450
Soups (avg.)	130
Spaghetti (1 C)	195
Spinach (1 C)	40
Strawberries (1 C)	100
Sugar (1 tspn)	30
Syrups (avg.)	50
Tea	1
Tomatoes (1)	35
Tuna fish (4 oz)	225
Turkey (6 oz)	300
Veal (6 oz)	450
Waffles (1)	215
Watermelon	25
Yogurt (1 C)	120

L E S S O N 10

The "Final Solution" and its Perpetrators

Reading 10A

ARRIVAL IN AUSCHWITZ

"You have 15 minutes. Pack one suitcase and report in front of your house."

You and your family join a procession marching to the railroad station. You are guarded by SS men and local police. The train arrives—cattle cars. You hold your father's hand as you are forced into a car with 80 to 100 other people. The door slams and you hear the lock. About one-half hour later, the train begins to move.

After two hours, people grow thirsty; there is no room even to sit down; one small opening in a corner of the car is the sole source of air. There are no windows. It is almost impossible to see because of the darkness. You gasp for breath. There is no toilet, only a bucket somewhere in the middle of the car. The heat grows unbearable. Your father's hand has slipped from yours and you cannot see your family members. People begin to groan and scream, babies cry. The train stops—but nothing happens. Other trains pass by in a different direction.

The smell of sweat, excrement and urine permeates the car. People grow panicky, irritable, frantic. After eight hours, about 25 of the people have passed out or died. After 20 more hours, the train stops again. People cry out for water as they hear voices outside. A machine gun sprays the car and four people fall with blood flowing from their bodies. Your sister is one of them. Silence.

The doors open—air rushes in. "Raus! Raus! Out! Out!" There are dogs, men with guns. Prisoners in striped uniforms take suitcases, old people and the dead out of the car. You watch as they throw your sister's body onto a wagon. You move almost in a daze and get off the car onto the platform with crowds of others. Thousands of people have stumbled, fallen from the long line of cattle cars. The noises are deafening, frightening.

"Line up by fives! No talking!" Shots are heard. The air is filled with foul smelling smoke. A chimney is visible; flames and smoke billow from it. You are made to move in an endless line—shouts in German or other languages route people in different directions. Your father is again next to you. Someone whispers that you should lie about your age, "Tell them you're 16." A handsome SS man with a whip in his hand and his coat draped over his shoulders asks your age. "Sixteen," you lie. He points his whip to the left and you and your father follow his direction. You see your mother and old people and children going to the right. Unknown to you, you will never see them again. All those under 16 and over 40 are sent to die. Your mother, younger brothers and grandparents have disappeared.

There are lines, yelling, crying, dogs, orders, shots. Men and women have been separated from one another. You are made to strip and stand naked. Next, a bathhouse. You are sprayed with delousing solution—it burns. Still naked, you are marched to a long room where all body hair is shaved; your arm is tattooed with a number, and you are given an ill-fitting uniform and shoes. Finally, you are herded into a barracks with about 200 others.

What has happened? Where are we, you wonder. What has happened to your mother and brothers? Your father is silent; he seems to be hypnotized, stiff, not responding to anything around him. Where did they take your poor sister's body? You ask someone with a striped uniform, another prisoner, when you will see your mother and brothers again. Where are they? He roughly drags you to a window and points: "Do you see that chimney? Do you see the smoke? There are your mother and your brothers. This is not a summer camp—this is Auschwitz."

Questions

1. What do you think was the most frightening part of the deportation to, and arrival at, Auschwitz?

2. What is a "rite of passage"? Can you think of any examples of rites of passage that you have experienced or will experience?

3. If a rite of passage indicates a significant move from one phase of a person's life to another, such as from adolescence to adulthood, why is the cattle car experience considered a rite of passage?

4. As a result of the train transport, life has completely changed for the people on the videotape and the person in the essay. What has changed and how will life be different forever?

L E S S O N 11

Planet Auschwitz

HOLOCAUST CURRICULUM

Planet Auschwitz

USCHWITZ

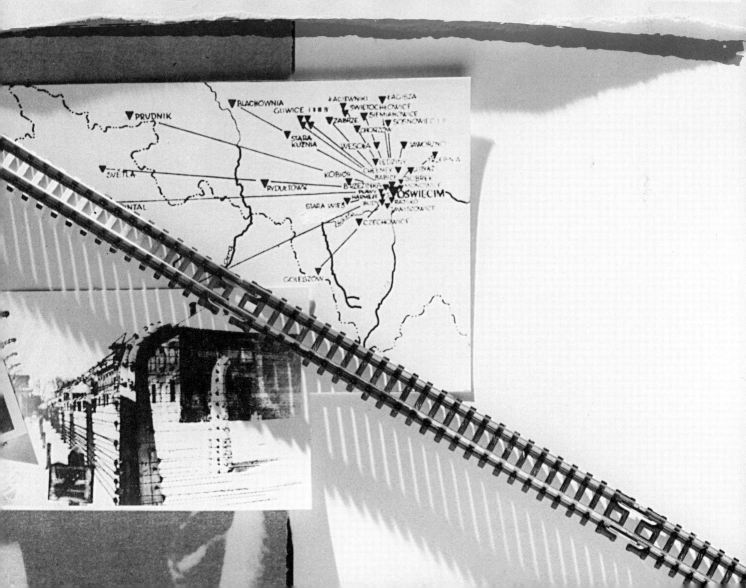

A "NORMAL" DAY IN AUSCHWITZ

As a 15-year-old girl, you have survived the selection on the platform. You are alone—packed into a barracks with hundreds of others but with no one from your family. You share your "bunk" with three bunkmates. The word "bunkmates" is not exactly correct—there are three other frightened, emaciated victims who share the wooden board on which you sleep.

4 a.m.: *Appel* or role call. Fall out, with only a prisoner's striped uniform and a pair of wooden shoes, into the biting zero-degree cold. Stand. One hour passes and a *Kapo*, a prisoner who is in charge of the barracks, calls numbers. Your number is called. All must wait because one person is not present. Fifteen minutes later, the body is dragged to its place. Even the dead must report. The *Kapo* yells his count to the SS guard: "All present or accounted for! One hundred ninety-four are standing, five are in the sick barrack, one is dead."

"Coffee"—dark water—and a slice of coarse bread are given to you as you stand in line. No one has been allowed to use the latrines. Three hours have passed, some people have urinated on themselves; finally, you are allowed to line up for the latrines. You are given three minutes in the large room with a mud floor and a series of cement slabs with holes in them. A prisoner is given a whip with which she beats women who take too long. An older woman confides to you that prisoners are found dead here each morning—suicides or drowned in excrement by someone else. The smell is overpowering, and you feel the urge to vomit. Yet, such smells are no longer new to you: the stench in the cattle car, the sickening odor of the smoke from the chimneys, the body smells of the prisoners crammed into the barracks and now this latrine smell. The older woman tells you that almost all the women have ceased menstruating—either from fear, malnutrition or disease.

Again the *Appelplatz* (role call place), where you see women being beaten for "slacking." You are chosen for a work detail at the *Brezhinka,* the mountain of clothing collected from victims, most of whom were gassed upon their arrival. Your job is to sort clothing. You are lucky—one can "organize," that is, steal extra clothes from here. Should you be caught, you will probably be beaten, or worse. As you work, you watch trains arrive, the chimneys of the crematoria belching flames, the lines of people at the gas chamber, the dogs barking, women crying, children screaming and SS men shouting commands.

At noon, you are given "coffee" and another slice of bread with margarine. Ten minutes to eat. Back to work. In the distance, you see men carrying cement blocks from one place to another. Later, they are made to carry them back. Every so often you hear gunshots. Everyone around you has the stench of death, disease and excrement. All are crawling with lice. The sky is gray, trees glisten with snow, icicles form on the barracks and on the barbed wire fences.

While you work at the *Brezhinka,* you suddenly find a familiar sweater, your mother's, and a pair of shoes—your sister's. They are dead, you know that now. You cannot stop to mourn or think of them. Guards are watching. You tear the sweater to pieces. It is a small act of defiance, of sabotage.

All prisoners move as if in a fog. Some are beaten, some are hung, shot or tortured—they seem to show no emotion because of their starved, semi-hypnotized condition. By 6 p.m., your head swims—malnutrition, grief, fear, pain, thirst—all take their toll.

Another *Appel.* Nineteen people have died from your group—a small number for this day— in the bitter cold.

After the final 'meal,' which consists of one slice of bread and a small piece of hard salami, you return to the barracks. People stare blankly. The *Kapo* grabs a young girl and beats her until blood pours from her head—the girl has not performed some simple task to the *Kapo's* satisfaction. She moans on the wooden floor. No one moves. The *Kapo* swears at the prisoners and storms into her room at the end of the barracks.

You lay on your board with two other girls (the third has not returned) thinking of your mother and sister in your kitchen at home and fall asleep.

THIS DAY IN AUSCHWITZ IS BASED ON TESTIMONIES FROM SURVIVORS OF AUSCHWITZ.

Using Readings 9C, "Daily Log," 9D, "Calorie Tally" and 11A, "A 'Normal' Day in Auschwitz," answer the following questions on a separate sheet of paper.

1. What things do you control in a normal day? What does the girl control?

2. What is controlled or determined by others during your day? What is controlled or determined by others in the girl's day?

3. What do you do with "free" time? What did the girl do with "free" time?

4 At what point in your day did your activities differ from the girl in Auschwitz?

5. Using Reading 9D, "Calorie Tally," calculate the number of calories the girl in Auschwitz consumed in a "normal" day. Then, calculate the number of calories you consume in a normal day.

LEGAL BRIEF: LIFE UNWORTHY OF LIFE

The man with the whip who stood calmly on the platform directing human traffic in "Arrival at Auschwitz" was the infamous Dr. Mengele. He and several other doctors were in charge of the selection process when prisoners arrived. They also supervised the selections that were carried out regularly at the roll calls and in the barracks. The purpose was to weed out "excess" or "unnecessary" people who were "non-productive." The term used by the Nazi doctors for these people was "life unworthy of life." It was borrowed from a medical book written in 1920 and became the phrase that allowed physicians to conduct horrible experiments on human beings and decide who would live and who would die. "Life unworthy of life" also best captures the heart of the Nazi philosophy toward the Jews and other unfortunate groups who became the victims of the Third *Reich.*

As early as 1933, respected physicians were involved in a program of sterilization—making people incapable of reproducing. The victims of this program were people whom the doctors decided were mentally deficient. The doctors' endorsement of this program then led to their support of the Nazi proposal for the killing of mentally and/or physically handicapped children, and then, mentally and/or physically handicapped adults in the so-called "euthanasia" program. "Euthanasia" is usually defined as "mercy killing." In Germany, in 1933, the term was applied to people who were considered "unworthy of life." The doctors believed that mental illness, drunkenness, other mental and physical disabilities could be passed on genetically. What mattered most to them was the so-called health of the "Aryan race." Consequently, they saw it as their duty to remove those who would, according to their theories, "weaken the race" through reproduction. Over 450,000 people were sterilized or killed in special institutes and hospitals before the program was ended. These places were often equipped with gas chambers.

After 1941, a state policy of "euthanasia" and forced sterilization easily changed into a state policy for mass murder. This policy was carried out in death camps like Treblinka and Auschwitz. Those subjected to gassing in the "euthanasia" program during the 1930s were said to have received "special treatment," *Besonderhandlung.* The same phrase would be used as a euphemism, a substitute word to hide the real meaning, to refer to gassing of Jews in death camps. The doctors who had formerly worked in the special hospitals of the "euthanasia" and sterilization programs now appeared at the death camps. The first step for them was to assist the SS commandants of camps to reduce the "excess population" of their camps. But soon, doctors like Dr. Mengele, his superior, Dr. Wirths, or the internationally known Dr. Clauberg were selecting people as guinea pigs for horrible experiments.

— Mengele tried to discover what determined eye color in twins by killing them and then dissecting the eyes.

— Wirths conducted experiments on women by unnecessarily removing portions of the uterus to examine what he called "pre-cancerous growths."

— Clauberg injected poisonous substances into the wombs of women and subjected men and women to radiation of their genitals, presumably for cancer research.

— A German pharmaceutical company sponsored a program in which German doctors injected people with typhus. The doctors later killed the victims by injecting a poisonous drug into their hearts. The bodies were then dissected for experimental research.

None of these experiments furthered medical research—yet, even if they had, the inhuman treatment of the prisoners was unjustifiable.

How did thousands of medical doctors become involved with the murder of the Jews? Were they forced? Were they threatened? Or did they truly believe the racial theories of the Nazis?

German doctors were not forced to participate in the sterilization, the "euthanasia" or the mass murder programs. They were not threatened if they refused (as some did). Some seemed to have believed in the Nazi genetic theories. Many tried to impress their superiors or gain favor with politically powerful Nazis by doing research about breeding a "super-race" (biological engineering). Rarely had doctors had such opportunities for human experimentation. To experiment with animals and write or lecture about it was one thing, but to experiment directly on humans was quite another—a shortcut to acclaim and a more "glamorous" type of research. All hoped to advance their careers; a few were fanatical Nazis.

Despite this career building, each of those thousands of doctors had taken the Hippocratic Oath and had pledged to "heal the sick" and protect life: "I will follow that method of treatment which . . . I consider for the benefit of my patients and abstain from whatever is deleterious and mischievous. I will give no deadly medicine to anyone if asked, nor suggest any such counsel . . . I will . . . benefit the sick and abstain from every voluntary act of mischief and corruption."

Having solemnly taken that ancient oath, how was it possible that those physicians participated in the selections at Auschwitz and the other camps? Was that participation "deleterious" and against the benefit of human life? And was participating in medical experiments literally giving "deadly medicine"?

Historians have suggested some partial explanations for the behavior of the Nazi doctors. *The first of these explanations comes from understanding the nature of "Planet Auschwitz."* It was, in almost every sense, another world. In such an environment, all established codes of right and wrong were abandoned. Accepted moral values and ethical rules—standards of behavior—were not applicable. Personalities seemed to change to match the environment. At Auschwitz, anything was possible.

Dr. Mengele was the most infamous of those doctors at Auschwitz. Before the Holocaust, he was involved with scientific research and saw himself as a scientist. He was described by other doctors as "cold and heartless," "completely dependable," "equal to any task" and "honest and trustworthy."

At Auschwitz, some prisoners described him as kind to children—yet, they knew he was responsible for the torturous experiments performed mainly on children. One survivor noted that the Gypsy children often called him "Uncle Mengele." She then recalled how after bringing candy to some children he would take them away to be killed and dissected. He committed open and deliberate murder.

The second explanation concerning the behavior of the doctors is related to the concept of the Volksgemeinschaft or racial community of people, the "Aryan race." The doctors believed that their first responsibility was to preserve the health of the "Aryan race." The *Volksgemeinschaft* was defined as a single body, and parasites or infections like Gypsies, Jews and others were said to weaken it. The doctors described the *Volksgemeinschaft* as their most important "patient." The removal of "undesirables" from that "patient" was the primary method used to guarantee its health. The doctors of the Third *Reich* claimed that mental illness, drunkenness, ugliness, body disfigurement and other mental and physical disorders were hereditary. They also claimed that forms of behavior could be inherited. According to the definitions of Jews in laws passed in 1933, 1934 and 1935, Jewishness was also hereditary. All these genetic theories allowed medical murder to proceed.

Reichsfuehrer SS Himmler was convinced of the "moral necessity" of experiments on humans and the murder of "non-productive" or "undesirable" groups. He said: "All who still reject human experiments are committing high treason." He agreed to support the medical experiments and to accept full responsibility for them in the name of the *Fuehrer* and the Third *Reich*.

Advancing careers, abandoning all previous standards of behavior, belief in racial theories, total support from the authorities and no opposition from any leading scientific or medical institution all contributed to the doctors' participation in the "Final Solution." These same elements made it easier for those in other professions to participate, too. Such behavior, by civilized and educated people, could occur because of their failure to recognize the value of life for all human beings.

The key to the medical involvement in mass murder seems to have been the phrase "life unworthy of life." These men (and women) perceived their victims as less than human or as objects—dead matter. "Life unworthy of life" may summarize Auschwitz, the death camps, the Holocaust.

LESSON 12

Planet Auschwitz

THE DOCTOR'S TRIAL: A DRAMATIZATION

(Student booklet, reading 11B, "Legal Brief: Life Unworthy of Life," provides some background for this trial. The text for this exercise is based on the transcripts of the *Trials of War Criminals Before the Nuernberg Military Tribunals: "The Medical Case,"* Vols. I, II.)

Participants:

>Presiding Judge
>Defendant (Dr. Schultz): person on trial
>Defense Lawyer: represents the Defendant
>Prosecuting Lawyer: represents the Allied Governments, which
>are accusing the Defendant of war crimes
>A Witness (Dr. Bauer)
>A Witness (Dr. Wald)
>Jury Foreman (Teacher)
>Jury (the rest of the class)

JUDGE: After the defeat of Germany in World War II, the Allies—France, Great Britain, the Soviet Union and the United States—decided to set up an international court or tribunal to bring the leading Nazi criminals to justice. The Nazis were accused of war crimes and crimes against humanity. The trials began in 1946 in the German city of Nuremberg. Some of those tried were doctors. Other trials took place in Germany in 1963, 1970 and 1980. We are here today to conduct a trial to determine the guilt or innocence of Dr. Schultz, a former Nazi doctor.

What I am about to read to you is from the Hippocratic Oath, an oath that all doctors take upon graduating from medical school. This oath will be used as one of the standards to judge guilt or innocence in this trial:

I swear that . . . I will keep this oath:

I will follow that method of treatment which, according to my ability and judgment, I consider for the benefit of my patients, and abstain from whatever is deleterious and mischievous. I will give no deadly medicine to anyone if asked, nor suggest any such counsel . . . With purity and with holiness I will pass my life and practice my art . . . Into whatever houses I will enter I will go into them for the benefit of the sick and will abstain from every voluntary act of mischief and corruption . . .

JUDGE: Dr. Schultz, you are accused of medical crimes—of participating in the so-called "Euthanasia Program" from 1939 to 1941 and of conducting medical experiments on human beings in 1942 and 1944, which caused their deaths. How do you plead to this indictment, that is, to these charges?

(Dr. Schultz stands and faces the Judge.)

DR. SCHULTZ: Not guilty in the sense of the indictment.

JUDGE: Could you explain, please?

DR. SCHULTZ: I conducted medical experiments at several concentration camps— Buchenwald {boo-khen-vald}, Gross-Rosen, Neuengamme {noi-en-gahm} and Auschwitz—but do not consider these experiments criminal. Nor do I consider my participation in the Euthanasia Program to be a crime.

(Dr. Schultz is seated.)

JUDGE: Mr. Prosecutor, you may begin your examination of the witnesses.

PROSECUTOR: I would like to call Dr. Bauer to the witness stand. *(Dr. Bauer takes the stand.)*

PROSECUTOR: Dr. Bauer, were you a physician at Auschwitz?

DR. BAUER: I was, and I was there at the same time as Dr. Schultz.

PROSECUTOR: Did you participate in selections on the platform at Auschwitz?

DR. BAUER: Even though the selections were always considered a medical matter, I did not participate in them. When I arrived at Auschwitz, my supervisor instructed me to observe a selection. I watched and vomited. I could not believe what was happening. I refused to take part in such duty.

PROSECUTOR: Were you punished?

DR. BAUER: No. At first, Dr. Wirths and then Dr. Mengele tried to convince me of the necessity of having doctors conduct the selections. I gave excuses—I said I had too much work, that emotionally I could not tolerate being a part of the selections. Finally, they let me be. The next doctor who arrived had a similar experience—getting sick and refusing. He was an ardent Nazi who believed in the inferiority of the Jews and saw them as subhumans. But even he was upset. Yet, after two weeks under the teaching and advice of Dr. Mengele, he was working the platform with the other doctors. To my knowledge, there were a few other doctors who successfully refused to participate in the selections and some who would not participate in the experiments.

PROSECUTOR: Did you participate in medical experiments on human subjects—on the prisoners of the camps?

DR. BAUER: I did not. I refused after voicing my objections to Dr. Schultz and the other SS physicians. I told him that I could not be a party to experiments that were governed solely by "biological thought."

PROSECUTOR: Could you explain what you mean by that?

DR. BAUER: By biological thought, I mean that the physician sees the subject or patient as an object or thing. He does not see the patient as a human being. For him, the human relationship no longer exists, and a man or woman becomes a mere object—like a mail package. In that doctor's judgment, the subject is a machine, a *biological* mechanical object— something like a living robot. But a physician is not supposed to make such judgments. His task is to care for the sick.

PROSECUTOR: Thank you, Dr. Bauer.

JUDGE: Mr. Defense Lawyer, do you have any questions?

DEFENSE LAWYER: Thank you, Your Honor. Dr. Bauer, weren't the experiments authorized by the state?

DR. BAUER: Yes.

DEFENSE: And isn't it true that if the state authorizes certain acts, the individual should obey?

DR. BAUER: Between the state order and the doctor stands the human conscience. A doctor has taken the Hippocratic Oath, which insists that he uphold that conscience. That oath forbids him to harm his patient. Thus, for the doctor, the idea of people as individuals is more important than some concept of the nation or race.

DEFENSE: Do you agree that since the state authorized medical experiments, the state also assumed responsibility for the actions of a physician?

DR. BAUER: In this case, we are talking about the state—Germany—authorizing a medical program of murder—administered by doctors. They administered this program to protect what they called the *Volksgemeinschaft*. The *Volksgemeinschaft* was considered the racial community of the German people, the Aryan race. Safeguarding the racial community became a basis for doctors' activities. They used this theory to justify a policy of medical extermination.

But I do not believe the state can assume the responsibility for a physician to his patients or to experimental subjects. The Hippocratic Oath is still the doctor's Golden Rule.

DEFENSE: You may step down.

(Dr. Bauer is seated.)

PROSECUTOR: I call Dr. Schultz to the stand.

(Dr. Schultz takes the stand.)

PROSECUTOR: Dr. Schultz, could you tell me how the "euthanasia" decisions were made?

DR. SCHULTZ: At first, every German mental institution received questionnaires from the Reich Ministry of the Interior. These questionnaires were to be completed for each inmate of the institution and sent back to the Ministry. The doctors at the institutions had to fill out the questionnaires, and a panel of experts would examine the photocopies of them in Berlin. Each of three doctors on the panels received copies and independently decided which of the subjects should be treated.

PROSECUTOR: When you say "treated," you mean killed?

DR. SCHULTZ: Yes.

PROSECUTOR: Were only mentally ill patients killed?

DR. SCHULTZ: No. In 1940, the experts—the doctors—*we*—extended our procedures to inmates of concentration camps. Those inmates, like Polish prisoners of war and Gypsies, who were selected by camp doctors, were also sent to the euthanasia centers.

PROSECUTOR: What was a "euthanasia center"?

DR. SCHULTZ: Hospitals or medical centers that had been designated for the euthanasia treatments. They were especially equipped for this duty: some had gas chambers, others had drug facilities for special treatment.

PROSECUTOR: Were Jews and non-Germans included?

DR. SCHULTZ: Yes. The program also included homosexuals and mentally and physically deficient children. The questionnaires were filled out by doctors or officials of local health departments, heads of children's clinics, physicians, regular hospitals, etc. Later still, workers from Poland, Czechoslovakia, Hungary, Roumania and other eastern territories who had become unfit for work were executed as part of the program, too. All those people were a burden to the institutions or the prisons or the labor camps. They served no function.

PROSECUTOR: How many questionnaires might a doctor review in a day?

DR. SCHULTZ: Oh, between two and three hundred.

PROSECUTOR: Let me draw your attention to Exhibit A, the Registration Form—the questionnaire you mentioned. Why was it necessary to include a category for "Race"?

DR. SCHULTZ: The Euthanasia Program was for the good of the *Volksgemeinschaft,* the German people. We had to know the race and nationality of each subject. Non-Aryans were potential threats to the purity and health of German blood and had to be removed—like an infection or a cancer.

PROSECUTOR: Let me draw your attention to the category of "Value of work." Why was that included?

DR. SCHULTZ: In many cases, the decisions on life or death did not depend on the degree of insanity. Some were kept alive because they could do work. Productivity, after all, was a major goal—especially during the war. Patients who had tuberculosis, cancer or other weakening illnesses were included in the Euthanasia Program. They were in the category of "useless eaters" and were often starved to death because food was necessary for our soldiers and our healthy Aryans. Anyone unfit for work was a candidate for euthanasia.

PROSECUTOR: Did this category include sick children?

DR. SCHULTZ: Of course, because they could not work. We would often consult with parents and suggest to them that we could cure the child at our special institutions. They would be informed later that the child had died.

PROSECUTOR: How did you happen to be at Auschwitz and the other camps?

DR. SCHULTZ: Many of the staff of the Euthanasia Program were assigned to work on the "Final Solution."

PROSECUTOR: Can you explain why?

DR. SCHULTZ: We had learned much. We knew the most efficient ways to dispose of large numbers of useless beings. One of our doctors perfected the use of gas chambers. His plans were used in the construction of the gas chambers at Auschwitz and other camps. Adolf Eichmann, in charge of the Jewish Deportation Department, approved of the methods used in the Euthanasia Program. No one had any objections to doing away with those Jews who were unable to work. By 1942, our method had been well-tested. Everyone seemed pleased that such medical efficiency could be brought to the important task of killing useless people.

PROSECUTOR: If killing was such an important task, why did you engage in medical experiments?

DR. SCHULTZ: These experiments were for the good of the people of Germany. I, myself, was involved primarily in typhus research and assisted in the sterilization program. I worked on mass sterilization experiments. These included using X-rays and castration.

PROSECUTOR: No further questions.

JUDGE: Mr. Defense Lawyer, do you have any questions?

DEFENSE: Dr. Schultz, why did you participate in the Euthanasia Program?

DR. SCHULTZ: My task as a German physician was the well-being and health of the *Volksgemeinschaft*. What else could matter? I was engaged in strengthening the only patient that could matter to me—my *Volk*. Even if this were not my primary concern, we were entering an age in which defectives—useless people, life unworthy of life—would endanger all of us. These were not whole people—they were not full human beings. The future generations of the Aryan race—my grandchildren—were depending on me to do the right thing.

There is more to my involvement. Euthanasia was decreed by the *Fuehrer*. The law was passed in 1933. For a doctor to refuse to participate was to disobey the law and ignore his responsibility to the future. The law is the law.

DEFENSE: No further questions.

JUDGE: You may step down.

(Dr. Schultz is seated.)

DEFENSE: I call Dr. Wald to the stand.

(Dr. Wald takes the stand.)

DEFENSE: Dr. Wald, were you a member of the medical staff at Auschwitz?

DR. WALD: Yes.

DEFENSE: Did you take part in the selections?

DR. WALD: Yes.

DEFENSE: Did you feel any reservations about this activity?

DR. WALD: At first, yes. Auschwitz was like nothing I had seen before—a different world. The conditions were horrendous: filth, lack of sanitation, lice, disease (especially typhus), dysentery and almost every sort of skin disorder, along with vitamin deficiencies and malnutrition. I had been a part of one of the euthanasia panels of medical experts. The selections at Auschwitz were very much like the selections in that program—but instead of seeing just registration forms (Exhibit A), we saw patients in front of us on the platform. In a sense, it was more ethical to make judgments based on our physical observations of the subjects. When Dr. Mengele explained the purpose of the selections more completely, I put my reservations aside. Some of the leading people in the medical profession were there, so why not me? If they did not object, if the leaders of the state did not object, why should I?

DEFENSE: No further questions.

JUDGE: Mr. Prosecutor, do you have any questions?

PROSECUTOR: Thank you, Your Honor. Dr. Wald, did you also participate in experiments?

DR. WALD: No. When I realized the purpose of the experimental laboratories, and that the prisoners were not volunteers, and that many suffered greatly and almost all died, I simply refused to conduct such experiments.

PROSECUTOR: Were you punished in any way for this choice?

DR. WALD: No. I was allowed to make my own decision. I worked in the infirmary alongside some of the Jewish prisoner doctors. I considered them good colleagues.

PROSECUTOR: Yet, during the selections, you were willing to send them to their deaths?

DR. WALD: That was different. Besides, I did not send any doctors to the gas—at least not that I know about. These Jews were partly responsible for the horrible conditions in the camp because there were so many of them. They carried lice off the trains and even the disinfectant showers did not clear up that problem. They were a threat to us and to the other prisoners. Further, our goal was the same as it had been in the Euthanasia Program: to improve the Aryan race, guarantee the *Volksgemeinschaft* of its continued existence. We wanted to strengthen it. The Jews had clearly weakened the *Volk* and had brought about their own fate. Didn't they control the medical profession? Didn't they anger good Germans with their control of the economy, the banks, businesses and stock market? We were doing the will of the community—eliminating Jews.

PROSECUTOR: Did you know for certain that Jews controlled all those things? Did you know Jews who controlled banks and businesses?

DR. WALD: No, I didn't know any. I had several Jewish friends—mostly doctors. They were good men and excellent doctors.

PROSECUTOR: On what basis, then, did you think they controlled German society?

DR. WALD: Well, it was common knowledge.

PROSECUTOR: So you decided to help kill them?

DR. WALD: I was engaged in a state-ordained policy. I, myself, would not kill anyone—I believe in the words of the great German founder of modern medicine, Paracelsus: "The doctor grows with his heart, he comes from God and is enlightened by Nature—the best of all drugs is Love."

PROSECUTOR: So you killed Jews because you loved them?

DR. WALD: Of course not. I loved the most important patient—the German *Volk*. Besides, I did not personally kill anyone. And I refused to hurt anyone— I refused to aid in experiments, even though my career would have been greatly advanced if I had agreed to participate.

PROSECUTOR: Dr. Wald, what do you think of Dr. Schultz?

DR. WALD: An excellent scientist. He was formal but kind. He had a good reputation among doctors and was even respected by the prisoners. The children were fond of him.

PROSECUTOR: Did he kill children?

DR. WALD: He experimented with children—his typhus experiments.

PROSECUTOR: Tell us about those experiments.

DR. WALD: Thousands of prisoners were purposely infected with typhus bacteria. This was done by exposing open wounds to lice. The most successful method, however, was to inject already infected blood into a healthy patient. In fact, a supply of prisoners was kept in the infirmary just for the purpose of drawing their infected blood to give to subjects for the experiments.

PROSECUTOR: Did those suppliers live long?

DR. WALD: Of course not, but they were easily replaced. I could not bring myself to inject children or healthy subjects, so I refused.

PROSECUTOR: What was the purpose of such experiments?

DR. WALD: To develop a vaccine for typhus.

PROSECUTOR: Was such a vaccine developed?

DR. WALD: No.

PROSECUTOR: Had it been developed, would you have approved of the method, that is, of using human subjects in that way?

DR. WALD: I did not participate. I do not condemn Dr. Schultz, but I personally would not have allowed such experiments. There is a limit to such research.

PROSECUTOR: You are excused. I call Dr. Schultz back to the stand.

(Dr. Wald is seated and Dr. Schultz takes the stand.)

PROSECUTOR: Dr. Schultz, how could you, as a doctor of medicine who swore the Oath of Hippocrates, commit acts of murder in the so-called "Euthanasia Program" and in the death camps?

DR. SCHULTZ: I repeat: the state had ordered those programs. They were for the salvation of the German *Volk* and, in a sense, were self-defense. My goal was to obtain results. I did not consider the experiments or the euthanasia decisions to be murder. We were giving a special treatment to the ill, the lazy, the ugly, the useless eaters. This may be a radical solution to the problem of the health of the community—but it works. I did not deal with people, but with blood cells, with registration forms, with categories, just as doctors all over the world do. I see no contradiction between my actions and my oath. I had nothing against individual Jews; I am a doctor, after all, and committed to healing and, as my colleague said, to love. The Jews were a potential help to curing typhus—or other diseases like tuberculosis. I helped with experiments on Jewish children who were injected with tuberculosis. They were hanged after several weeks so their lungs could be dissected. The other doctor who conducted those experiments has saved lives since the war in his own private tuberculosis clinic. Although he killed twenty children during the war, he has saved at least twenty-one lives since then. Perhaps those he saved benefitted from his earlier experiments on people.

JUDGE: Do you think you have committed crimes?

DR. SCHULTZ: Absolutely not. I obeyed the state and my beliefs. We doctors were systematic, professional and organized. We even gave subjects injections of morphine so they would feel nothing. All we did was kill them.

Auschwitz gave us the opportunity to carry out a government policy that we believed in. We doctors were the rulers of the camp: professional, meticulous technicians authorized by the highest officials to conduct whatever experiments we saw fit. The only law in Auschwitz was work: if you could not work, what was the use of your life? A clean moral system. To survive at Auschwitz, you had to be worthy of life—able to work. Life unworthy of life—the useless ones, the inferior ones, the ones who would have polluted our race—was not allowed to exist.

PROSECUTOR: You may step down.

(Prosecutor and Dr. Schultz are seated.)

JUDGE: You must now decide if the defendant, Dr. Schultz, is guilty of
(TO THE JURY)   crimes against humanity. Your verdict must be based solely on the evidence presented in the "Legal Brief" and this trial. In reaching your verdict, consider whether or not Dr. Schultz had obligations toward the following:

— the Oath of Hippocrates
— established moral principles, that is, generally accepted
    standards of right and wrong
— German law

You may deliberate out loud, but your votes must be by secret ballot and be justified with a written argument. The Jury Foreman may now conduct the deliberations.

Reading 12B

EXHIBIT A: REGISTRATION FORM

Number _____

      Name of Institution: _____

      At: _____

Surname and Christian name of the patient: _____

Date of birth: _____ Place: _____ District: _____

Last place of residence: _____ District: _____

Marital status: _____

Religion: _____ Race*: _____

Previous profession: _____ Nationality: _____

Army service when? 1914-1918 or from 1-9-1939: _____

War injury: _____

Address of next of kin: _____

Regular visits and by whom (address): _____

Guardian or nurse (name, address): _____

Responsible for payment: _____

Since when in institution: _____ Since when ill: _____

Twin? Yes/No _____ Blood relatives of unsound mind: _____

Diagnosis: _____

Clinical description (previous history, course, condition; in any case ample data regarding mental condition):

_____

Very restless? Yes/No: _____ Bedridden? Yes/No: _____

Incurable physical illness: Yes/No (which) _____

Schizophrenia: Fresh attack _____ Final condition _____

Good recovery _____

Mental debility: Weak _____ Imbecile _____ Idiot _____

Epilepsy: Psychological alteration _____ Avg. frequency _____

Therapeutics (insulin, cardiazol, malaria, Salvarsan, etc.) permanent result: _____

Crime: _____ Former punishable offenses: _____

Manner of employment (detailed description of work): _____

_____

Permanent/temporary employment, independent worker? Yes/No _____

Value of work (if possible compared with average performance of healthy person): _____

_____

                        _____ Place, Date _____

                Signature of the head doctor or his representative (doctors who are not psychiatrists or neurologists, please state same).

* German or of similar blood (of German blood), Jew,
  Jewish mixed breed Grades I or II, Negro (mixed breed).

(Medical Trials, Vol. II, p. 850)

JUROR'S BALLOT

You must now decide if the defendant, Dr. Schultz, is guilty of crimes against humanity. Your verdict must be based solely on the evidence presented in the "Legal Brief" and this trial.

☐ GUILTY

☐ NOT GUILTY

Justify your verdict. In justifying your verdict, consider whether or not Dr. Schultz had obligations toward the following:

— the Oath of Hippocrates
— established moral principles, that is, generally accepted
standards of right and wrong
— German law

_____

_____

_____

_____

_____

_____

_____

_____

_____

_____

_____

_____

Reading 12D

RESCUE IN DENMARK

Denmark was invaded and occupied by the German Army *(Wehrmacht)* {ver-mahcht} in the spring of 1940. Since there was little resistance by the Danish people, the Danish government was allowed to continue to function. This government refused to carry out German anti-Jewish laws.

In the fall of 1943, an extraordinary event occurred. The German destruction machinery was halted in Denmark. The Danish civil service and a whole population determined to rescue the Jews refused to cooperate with the Germans. On September 18, 1943, Hitler decided that the Danish Jews would be deported to Auschwitz. No Danish police or armed forces would cooperate. They refused to round up the approximately 6,500 Danish Jews. SS troops had to be sent from Germany to Denmark because even the *Wehrmacht* commander, General Von Hanneken, refused to obey. He argued that the task of rounding up Jews was not a military one.

On the occasion of the Jewish New Year, September 28, 1943, news of an SS deportation round-up was announced to Jewish congregations in the synagogues. Two nights later, the *Gestapo,* the SS police, went door to door to round up Jews. Breaking into homes was, of course, against Danish law. The Danish police had threatened armed resistance if the SS broke the law. Thus, if Jews did not answer their doors, the SS moved on! Only 477 Jews were caught and sent to Theresienstadt {Ter-e-zen-shtet} (a concentration camp in Czechoslovakia) from which they were sent to Auschwitz.

On October 4, 1943, the Swedish government promised to grant sanctuary, a safe place, to Danish Jews. It led to one of the most remarkable rescues in history. First, doctors, teachers, businessmen, students, housewives, farmers, taxi drivers, etc., mobilized the Danish fishing fleet to take Jews across the Sund, the body of water separating Sweden from Denmark. Next, they moved Jews secretly to beaches and ports of departure. They raised money to pay for the crossing (about $100 per person); Danish police stood guard to ward off danger; taxi drivers drove Jews to the ports so as not to arouse suspicion; druggists supplied free stimulants to keep people awake all night. By the end of October, Denmark had rescued 7,220 Jews (including over 800 German Jewish refugees who had come to Denmark before 1940) and 686 non-Jewish spouses of Jews.

L E S S O N 13

The Rescuers

HOLOCAUST CURRICULUM

RESCUERS

THE VOICES OF CONSCIENCE

SALONIKA, GREECE: After Greece was occupied by the Germans in 1941, the Nazis requested the head Greek Orthodox priest to hand over a list of Jews in that city. The priest told the SS he could identify only Greeks, without any religious distinction.

What do you think happened?

MINSK, RUSSIA: Wilhelm Kube {kew-beh}, Nazi *Generalkommissar* of White Russia (central, western district of Russia), repeatedly refused to allow mass murders of Jews who had been deported from Germany to Minsk. Although Kube protected German Jews, he had fewer qualms about killing Russian Jews. While he did not vigorously object to the murder of Russian Jews, he objected to any brutal and inhumane treatment of the Jews while they were alive.

What do you think happened?

AUSCHWITZ, POLAND: Several SS physicians refused to participate in medical experiments on Auschwitz prisoners.

What do you think happened?

EUROPE: There are many examples of Nazis who refused to participate in the killing process; some members of the SS would not be a party to mass shootings; some Nazi Party members would not engage in anti-Jewish activities.

What do you think happened?

A LABOR CAMP NEAR AUSCHWITZ, POLAND: Seeing that a 15-year-old boy had been badly beaten while working on a cement detail, a German civilian engineer, who was an I.G. Farben supervisor, detoured him from his way to the infirmary where he would have died. The engineer hid the boy each day for the next three days so that the boy could rest.

What do you think happened?

WARSAW, POLAND: A Polish girl was visited one night by a Jewish friend who pleaded to be hidden from the Nazis. Although the Polish girl knew that hiding Jews might mean death for her and her family, she took her in.

What do you think happened?

UKRAINE: In 1941, an old farmer discovered a family of four Jews hiding in his barn. His young wife was extremely superstitious and anti-Semitic, but he was a devout Christian and believed it was a sin to murder Jews. He offered the family refuge in the loft of his barn. He told his wife to say nothing to anyone—not even his young children.

What do you think happened?

DENMARK: Although the German Army occupied Denmark from 1940 on, Danish officials from King Christian X to railroad employees to police officers all refused to cooperate with the Gestapo. They would not identify Jews and refused to introduce anti-Jewish measures of any kind.

What do you think happened?

RAOUL WALLENBERG: Raoul Wallenberg (1912-?) was a Swedish diplomat who saved thousands of Jews in Hungary during the Holocaust. He prevented their deportation to concentration and death camps during the German occupation of Hungary in the spring and summer of 1944.

Wallenberg was born in Stockholm, Sweden. His family was wealthy and included bankers, diplomats and industrialists. He traveled widely as a youth and could speak several languages. He studied architecture and city planning at the University of Michigan and graduated from there in 1935. He then worked for a business firm in South Africa and for a Dutch bank in Haifa, Palestine, where he met Jewish refugees from Germany in the late 1930s.

In 1944, he was working with the Swedish consulate in Budapest, Hungary. As a neutral country, Sweden could offer refuge for those who claimed Swedish citizenship. Wallenberg placed thousands of Jews in buildings under Swedish government authority where they were protected from the Nazis. He also distributed counterfeit passports and identification papers to thousands more who were scheduled for deportation to Auschwitz. With the forged papers secured by Wallenberg, these Hungarian Jews were given legal status as Swedish citizens, and thereby saved.

What do you think happened to him?

OSKAR SCHINDLER: Oskar Schindler was a member of the Nazi Party and a German businessman. Prior to the war, he had a reputation as a womanizer and heavy drinker. During the war, he was put in charge of a German factory near Kracow, Poland, to produce utensils for the German Army. In 1940, he employed 150 Jewish workers; by 1942, he employed 500. As the SS began to deport Jews to death camps, Schindler worked to protect them. He brought and kept whole families together, including old and "unproductive" people. He would often socialize with SS Commandant Goeth {get}, one of the most sadistic and murderous of the camp commanders. Through this socializing, however, he was able to save Jews, once even playing cards with Goeth for the life of a Jewish woman who worked in Goeth's house. Through his connections with high-ranking SS officials and businessmen, Schindler was able to secure extra food and medical supplies for his workers.

By 1944, Schindler was able to provide over 1,000 Jews with work cards that saved them from deportation to Auschwitz. He called them "his" Jews, and they all recognized that it was his personal courage that was keeping them alive. He continued to bribe SS guards and buy extra rations through illegal channels. When the Germans retreated from Eastern Poland in 1944, they took apart their factories and killed Jewish workers. Schindler managed to save his workers by transferring them as a group to another factory in Western Czechoslovakia.

What do you think happened to him?

WARSAW, POLAND: In October 1942, a group of non-Jewish fighters in the Polish underground led by Colonel Henryk Wolinski and a Jew, Adolf Berman, formed the organization known as *Zegota*. It was devoted to rescuing Jews in Warsaw and Kracow.

L E S S O N 14

The Rescuers

Reading 14A

Questions

1. Did Corrie ten Boom do the right thing when she lied to the Germans?

2. Was it right for the ten Booms to offer their house as a hiding place for Jews?

THE SECRET ROOM

(From Corrie ten Boom, *The Hiding Place* and Alan L. Lockwood, *The Secret Room in Holland*.)

In May 1940, Germany invaded the Netherlands. In only five days, the small nation was conquered. Approximately 140,000 Jews lived in Holland at this time. By January 1941, all Dutch were ordered to register and were issued identity cards. The cards issued to Dutch Jews had a "J" on them. In May 1942, Jews were ordered to wear a large, yellow six-pointed star with the word "Jew" printed in the center. Soon, the Germans began to round up Jews and send them to Auschwitz and other camps. Many Dutch protested against these and other anti-Jewish measures. The German reaction was swift and brutal: those who helped Jews were sent with them to the Nazi concentration camps.

Although she was not a Jew, 48 year old Cornelia ten Boom was profoundly affected by the "Final Solution." She would soon be facing the most difficult decisions of her life. Cornelia recalls how some of the Nazi rules and regulations affected the people of Haarlem, the city where she lived.

The curfew too, at first, was no hardship for us, since it was originally set at 10:00 P.M., long after we were indoors in any case. What we did object to were the identity cards each citizen was issued. These small folders containing photograph and fingerprints had to be produced on demand. A soldier or a policeman—the Haarlem police were now under the direct control of the German Commandant—might stop a citizen at any time and ask to see his card; it had to be carried in a pouch about the neck . . .

Early in the occupation Haarlemers were ordered to turn in all private sets (radios). Realizing it would look strange if our household produced none at all, we decided to turn in the portable and hide the larger, more powerful instrument in one of the many hollow spaces beneath the old twisting staircase.

Both suggestions were Peter's. He was sixteen at the time of the invasion and shared with other Dutch teenagers the restless energy of anger and impotence. Peter installed the table radio beneath a curve in the stairs just above Father's room and expertly replaced the old boards, while I carried the smaller one down to the big Vroom en Dreesman department store where the radio collection was being made. The army clerk looked at me across the counter.

"Is this the only radio you own?"

"Yes . . ."

He consulted a list in front of him. "Ten Boom, Casper, ten Boom, Elizabeth, at the same address. Do either of them own a radio?"

I had known from childhood that the earth opened and the heavens rained fire upon liars, but I met his gaze.

"No."

Only as I walked out of the building did I begin to tremble. Not because for the first time in my life I had told a conscious lie. But because it had been so dreadfully easy.

The hardships that the occupation caused for Corrie were minor compared to what happened to the Jewish citizens of Holland. Corrie had heard stories that Jews were being taken away in the night. Eventually, there were mass public arrests during the daytime.

Certainly public arrests, with no attempt to conceal what was happening, were becoming more frequent. One day as Father and I were returning from our walk we found the Grote Markt cordoned off by a double ring of police and soldiers. A truck was parked in front of the fish mart; into the back were climbing men, women, and children, all wearing the yellow star. There was no reason we could see why this particular place at this particular time had been chosen.

"Father! Those poor people!" I cried.

Not all of the Dutch people were as horrified as Corrie. Some of them joined the National Socialist Bond (NSB), an organization sympathetic to the Germans. Members of the NSB received extra benefits from the Germans: more food and clothing; better jobs and housing. The ten Boom family did not join the NSB. Instead, they became involved in the Dutch underground—an organization that helped hide and protect Jews.

Finding safe places for Jewish people was risky business. The ten Booms realized that if they were discovered they would be arrested and probably executed. Nonetheless, they believed their work was worth the risk.

The underground decided that a tiny, secret room should be built in the ten Boom house. It was to be in Corrie's bedroom. A Mr. Smit designed the hiding place.

He moved the heavy, wobbly old wardrobe away from the wall with surprising ease and pulled my bed into the center of the room. "This is where the false wall will go" Excitedly he drew out a pencil and drew a line along the floor thirty inches from the back wall. He stood up and gazed at it moodily.

"That's as big as I dare," he said. "It will take a cot mattress, though. Oh yes. Easily!"

Over the next few days he and his workmen were in and out of our house constantly. They never knocked. At each visit each man carried in something. Tools in a folded newspaper. A few bricks in a briefcase. "Wood!" he exclaimed when I ventured to wonder if a wooden wall would not be easier to build. "Wood sounds hollow. Hear it in a minute. No, no. Brick's the only thing for false walls."

After the wall was up, the plasterer came, then the carpenter, finally the painter. Six days after he had begun, Mr. Smit called Father, Betsie, and me to see.

We stood in the doorway and gaped. The smell of fresh paint was everywhere. But surely nothing in this room was newly painted! All four walls had that streaked and grimy look that old rooms got in coal-burning Haarlem. The ancient molding ran unbroken around the ceiling, chipped and peeling here and there, obviously undisturbed for a hundred and fifty years. Old water stains streaked the back wall, a wall that even I who had lived half a century in this room, could scarcely believe was not the original, but set back a precious two-and-a-half feet from the true wall of the building.

Mr. Smit stooped and silently pulled this panel up. On hands and knees Betsie and I crawled into the narrow room behind it. Once inside we could stand up, sit, or even stretch out one at a time on the single mattress. A concealed vent, cunningly let into the real wall, allowed air to enter from outside.

With his fist he struck the wall above the bookshelves. "The Gestapo could search for a year," he said. "They'll never find this one."

The ten Boom house with its secret room became the key point in a network that spread throughout Haarlem and into the countryside. Countless numbers of escaping Jews passed through the house on their way to other safe places. An illegal, secret telephone was installed so that communication could be maintained with other members of the underground. Elaborate procedures were established in case of a raid by the Gestapo; a raid that seemed inevitable given the increased activity in their house.

One procedure was designed to make sure that, in the event of a night raid, Corrie would not groggily give away the hiding place.

> Over and over again the group worked with me—Nils, Henk, Leendert—bursting into my room without warning, shaking me awake, hurling questions at me.
>
> The first time it happened I was sure the real raid had come. There was a terrific pounding on my door, then the beam of a flashlight in my eyes. "Get up! On your feet!" I could not see the man who was speaking.
>
> "Where are you hiding your nine Jews?"
>
> "We only have six Jews now."
>
> There was an awful silence. The room light came on to show Rolf clutching his head with his hands. "Oh no. Oh no," he kept saying. "It can't be that bad."
>
> "Think now," said Henk just behind him. "The Gestapo is trying to trap you. The answer is, "What Jews! We don't have Jews here."
>
> Gradually, with repeated drills, I got better. Still, when the time actually came, when they were real Gestapo agents really trained in getting the truth from people, how would I perform?

Indeed, the raid did come. Corrie was brusquely awakened by the Gestapo.

> "Tell me now, where are you hiding the Jews?" "I don't know what you're talking about . . ."
>
> "Where are the Jews?"
>
> "There aren't any Jews here."
>
> The man struck me hard across the face.
>
> "Where do you hide the ration cards?"
>
> "I don't know what you're—"
>
> The man hit me again. I staggered up against the astronomical clock. Before I could recover he slapped me again, then again, and again, stinging blows that jerked my head backward.
>
> "Where are the Jews?"
>
> Another blow.

"Where is your secret room?"

I tasted blood in my mouth. My head spun, my ears rang—I was losing consciousness.

Corrie was arrested but never revealed the location of the hiding place nor admitted that she had given aid to fleeing Jews. She was taken to a number of camps and prisons and suffered greatly both psychologically and physically. Eventually, she was taken to Ravensbruck, a concentration camp in Germany. For some reason, she was released. She revisited the camp in 1959 and discovered that her release was the result of an error made by a clerk, for a week after she left, all women her age were executed.

Despite Dutch aid to Jews and resistance to the Nazis, 110,000 of the Jews in the Netherlands were killed in the Holocaust.

L E S S O N 15
Resistance and Survival

HOLOCAUST CURRICULUM

RVIVAL

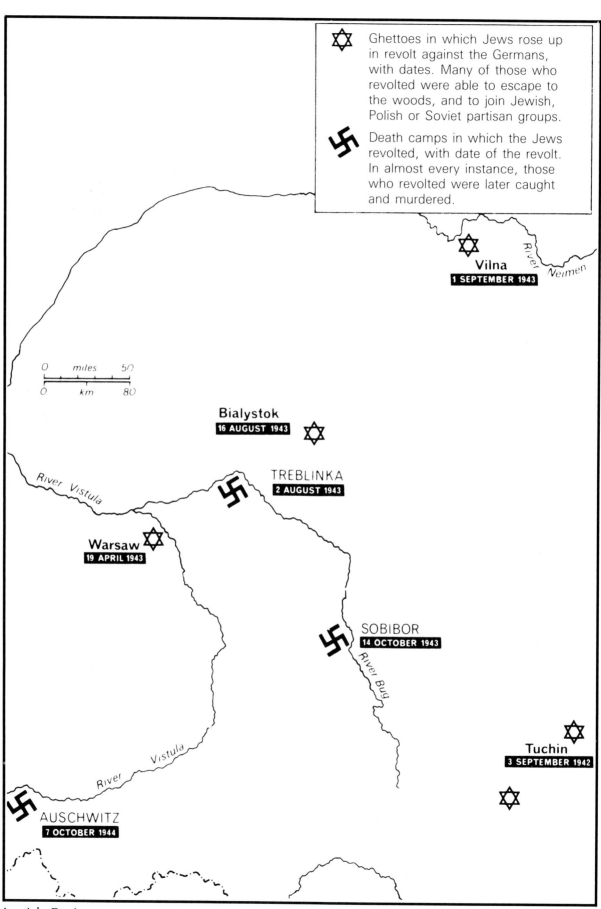

✡ Ghettoes in which Jews rose up in revolt against the Germans, with dates. Many of those who revolted were able to escape to the woods, and to join Jewish, Polish or Soviet partisan groups.

卐 Death camps in which the Jews revolted, with date of the revolt. In almost every instance, those who revolted were later caught and murdered.

River Neimen

✡ **Vilna**
1 SEPTEMBER 1943

0 miles 50
0 km 80

Bialystok
16 AUGUST 1943 ✡

River Vistula

卐 TREBLINKA
2 AUGUST 1943

✡ **Warsaw**
19 APRIL 1943

卐 SOBIBOR
14 OCTOBER 1943

River Bug

✡ **Tuchin**
3 SEPTEMBER 1942

✡

River Vistula

卐 AUSCHWITZ
7 OCTOBER 1944

Jewish Resistance

© Martin Gilbert 1982

Reading 15A

JEWISH ARMED RESISTANCE

PART I: THE QUESTION OF ARMED RESISTANCE

1. For Poland, the war is over. Germany has won. Polish cities are occupied. The Jewish and non-Jewish populations are subjected to laws imposed by the conquering Germans. People are still with their families—parents, grandparents, sisters and brothers. It is against the law to own any weapons, and guns are scarce. Recognizing all of these factors, consider carefully the following question.

Should the Jews have retaliated with violence at this point?

2. A Jewish ghetto is ordered to be formed. Jewish families are moved into apartments with other families. The average apartment now has 7.5 people per room.

Should the Jews have retaliated with violence at this point?

3. Food is rationed and forced labor begins. Anyone refusing to work will be imprisoned along with his family in a concentration camp.

Should the Jews have retaliated with violence at this point?

4. Within two weeks, starvation reduces the ranks of the Jewish population. Typhus is rampant along with dysentery. Sanitation facilities and running water are minimal. Lice, disease, hunger all produce hysterical, weakened and sick people. Within one month, most people have lost 30 to 40 pounds.

Should the Jews have retaliated with violence at this point?

5. Deportations begin and contrast is everywhere: dying, starving and sick victims contrast with healthy, strong, heavily armed SS men.

Should the Jews have retaliated with violence at this point?

6. Rumors continue to be heard that those who are deported have been resettled and are working. Post cards and letters have come back saying that life is hard but tolerable (no one in the ghetto knew that their relatives had been forced to write these postcards). On the one hand, there is fear for one's family members; on the other hand, there is hope for survival. No one expects a policy of annihilation.

Should the Jews have retaliated with violence at this point?

7. A train transport. Eighty people are jammed in a boxcar for three days without food or water. There are no sanitary facilities and barely enough air to breathe. This happens after prolonged starvation, slave labor, sickness, beatings, fear. People are totally demoralized.

The doors open—Auschwitz. Dogs, guns, yelling, crying, screams, smoke, the stench of burning flesh, family members slip away—a nightmare.

Should the Jews have retaliated with violence at this point?

8. Do you think asking: "Why didn't the Jews resist?" is an appropriate question in light of what you now know of the conditions during the Holocaust?

Also, family bonding worked against Jewish resistance. The *Gestapo* technique of holding the group responsible for individual actions stopped armed resistance. Whole communities were destroyed because of acts of armed resistance. One example is the Czech town of Lidice {*lid-i-say*}. After the assassination of Reinhard Heydrich in 1942, the Germans randomly chose the town of Lidice to be punished for this act. The men of Lidice were killed along with the children. The women were sent to concentration and labor camps. Such acts of brutality effectively stopped most armed resistance.

PART II: THE REALITY OF ARMED RESISTANCE

Given the conditions described in this lesson, the following examples seem nothing less than miraculous. (See map, p. 140, for each example.) Keep in mind the conditions that prisoners endured in the death camps, the near-total dehumanization and starvation described by survivors in the videotape and presented in other parts of this curriculum.

Ghettos:

■ Tuchin {*too-chin*} ghetto: On September 3, 1942, the Jewish community burned its homes and fled to the woods. The local Ukrainian populations hunted down all but 15 survivors of the 700 Jewish families and delivered them to the Germans.

■ Warsaw ghetto: On April 19, 1943, German troops surrounded the ghetto in order to begin the final deportations. Over 310,000 Jews had already been deported since June 1942. Almost all had been sent directly to the gas chambers at Treblinka. The Jewish Fighting Organization (ZOB), led by 23-year-old Mordechai Anielewicz {*ann-nee-lev-itch*}, consisted of about 1,500 young men and women. These young resistance fighters had lived in the ghetto for over two years and were nearly starved, suffering from disease and the sadness of having lost families and friends. In addition to these terrible conditions, they had managed to get only three light machine guns, about 100 rifles, a few dozen pistols, some hand grenades and explosives. When the resistors opened fire, the surprised German troops fled from the ghetto. The Warsaw Ghetto Rebellion had begun. It would last about one month.

The ZOB faced 3,000 German troops who were equipped with armored trucks, artillery, flame throwers, heavy machine guns and heavy explosives. The ZOB resisted until May 16, when the Great Synagogue was blown up and the ghetto, already in flames, was burned to the ground. Along with a few Polish non-Jews who had helped in the battle, 56,065 Jews surrendered. The prisoners were either shot, sent to Treblinka or Maidanek death camps or to labor camps where almost all died. Sixteen Germans had been killed. The Warsaw Ghetto Rebellion against the Germans was an utter failure from a military point of view. But word of it spread across Europe as a symbolic sign of hope for all those resisting the Nazis.

■ Bialystok {bee-al-eh-shtok} ghetto: On August 16, 1943, realizing the Nazis were going to destroy Bialystok, the ZOB attacked the Nazi forces. The battle lasted one day on the outskirts of the city. The resistors ran out of ammunition and were captured or killed. One group of young women carried on the struggle from within the ghetto and were eventually killed. Several other people escaped and joined partisans in the nearby forests.

■ Vilna ghetto: On September 1, 1943, largely because of increasing activity around the city, the Nazis moved to liquidate, that is, destroy, the ghetto. The United Partisan Organization (FPO), active for months, attempted an uprising within the ghetto. Poorly armed, they were hunted down and killed. Some escaped to the forests where they joined partisans until the liberation of Lithuania in July 1944.

Death Camps:

■ Treblinka: On August 2, 1943, after the camp had existed for one year, the 600 remaining Jews (800,000 had died there) blew it up and escaped to the nearby woods. Forty survived.

■ Sobibor: On October 14, 1943, armed with hatchets, Jewish prisoners and some Russian prisoners of war killed about a dozen Nazi officers. Four hundred prisoners, almost all who remained in the camp, rushed to the woods. Half died in a minefield surrounding the camp, and more were killed by Nazi and Polish Nazi groups. About sixty survived and joined Soviet partisans. Two days later, Himmler ordered Sobibor dismantled. The camp had been the site of the murder of over 250,000 Jews.

■ Auschwitz: On October 7, 1944, one of the *Sonderkommando* units, the special groups of prisoners used to clear the gas chambers of bodies, blew up one of the crematoria and attempted an armed escape. The members of this *Sonderkommando* were all killed.

Reading 15B

SURVIVAL AS RESISTANCE

Under unique circumstances like those of the Holocaust, "resistance" has to be redefined. Armed resistance was almost impossible—yet, it did occur. But another type of resistance became a way of life for Jews: to defeat death, from moment to moment and hour to hour. Even if survival was a result of what some survivors say was "pure luck," it represented resistance. Each day of survival meant successfully resisting the Nazi plan of genocide. To survive, to live, meant resistance.

As was apparent from "A 'Normal' Day in Auschwitz," the prisoners lost the freedom to make choices. To make choices was to act like a human being. One scholar has noted that committing suicide was one of the first signs of resistance by prisoners. They chose to die when they could make no choices about anything else. Some chose to attempt escape, although few succeeded. Survivors described small acts of "sabotage." Some at Auschwitz tore clothing apart as they sorted clothes in the *Brezhinka*. Others reported pouring sand into machinery they were forced to build in slave labor camps.

One prisoner of Auschwitz washed his hands in extremely filthy water each day. When another prisoner asked him why he bothered to "wash" in such water, he replied: "To prove to myself that I am still a human being." As he stood on the *Appelplatz* on his first full day in Auschwitz, a fourteen-year-old boy, alone after being separated from his family the day before, met an old man standing next to him. "What portion of the Bible were you studying at home?" the old man asked him. The boy told him. "We will begin reciting at that place today and go further each day," the old man whispered. "Why?" asked the boy. "To continue." Simple, routine or ritual acts became choices that allowed people to maintain links with their former lives.

Praying, one of the most serious "crimes" in any of the concentration, labor or death camps, was an act of resistance. Several survivors recall conducting secret religious services in the barracks. They risked their lives with this action but maintained their identity as Jews. This, to them, was resistance. One survivor of a labor camp recalled that on the Jewish Day of Atonement, *Yom Kippur,* she and many other prisoners chose to observe the religious tradition of fasting. When the SS guards discovered that these Jews were not eating, they forced them to do hours of punishing exercise. Then, those prisoners were not given rations for two days.

Those who survived have spoken of these acts as resistance—defeating the Nazi insistence that they become less than human.

The Nazis forced their victims to give up part of what it meant to be human: the freedom of choice. They tried to rob Jews of their human status.

Questions

1. What does "resistance" mean and why is it noble?

2. What are some examples of the different types of Jewish resistance during the Holocaust?

3. How is "survival as resistance" different than automatic antagonism toward authority?

4. Why do people resist?

Sounds of Silence:
World Responses

HOLOCAUST CURRICULUM

2,000,000 Jews Put To Death

LONDON, April 20 (INS)—The Nazis, since the start of the war, have slain 2,000,000 Jewish men, women and children and 5,000,000 other Jews are in immediate danger of extinction, the interallied information committee on occupied countries said today.

The 2,000,000, an eighth of the prewar Jewish world population, died in mass executions and through various forms of torture, the sixth report to be published by the committee said.

WORLD

The Railways and Deportation Routes

150

SUICIDE NOTE OF SHMUEL ZYGELBOIM {*zee-gull-boym*}

Shmuel Zygelboim had been an elected member of the Polish parliament before World War II. He represented the Jewish political party called the *Bund.* When Poland was conquered by Germany, the Polish government went into exile, that is, fled, to London. Zygelboim lived in London as part of the Polish government in exile. By 1943, he had learned of the massacres in Poland--in particular, in his city of Warsaw. After pleading for months with British government officials to make some public protest, he had achieved no success. Alone, desperate and depressed, he committed suicide on the steps of the British Parliament and left the following letter for the President of the Polish government in exile in London.

It has become clear from the information that has reached me from Poland that the Germans are now annihilating the remaining Jews of Poland with terrible cruelty. The last act of a tragedy without precedent in history is now being played out behind the walls of the ghetto. Responsibility for the crime of murdering the entire Jewish population of Poland lies first and foremost with the murderers themselves, but indirectly this responsibility lies with all mankind—the Allied nations and governments who have not yet made any effort toward concrete action to halt the crime . . .

I also wish to declare that even though the Polish government contributed much to awakening world public opinion, it did not do so in an adequate manner. It did nothing befitting the magnitude of the drama now taking place in Poland . . . I can no longer remain silent. I cannot live when the remnant of the Jewish people in Poland, whom I represent, is being steadily annihilated. My comrades in the Warsaw ghetto fell with weapons in their hands, in the last heroic struggle. I was not fortunate enough to die as they did and together with them. But I belong to them and to their mass graves. By my death I wish to express my vigorous protest against the apathy with which the world regards and resigns itself to the slaughter of the Jewish people.

Reading 16B

THE HOLOCAUST AND WORLD WAR II

The Holocaust was not the same as World War II. Hitler's first goal was to acquire "Lebensraum," or living space. His second goal was to make Germany "Judenrein," or clean of Jews. Hitler gained *Lebensraum* when the Third *Reich* expanded beyond Germany and throughout Europe in World War II. He also gained control of millions of Jews.

Mass murder became Hitler's goal because it became a possible "solution" to the question of how to get rid of the Jews.

The murder of the Jews could occur because during World War II the Germans occupied all of Europe. They, therefore, gained the freedom to do as they wished to 3,350,000 Jews in Poland, 600,000 Jews in Hungary, 765,000 Jews in Roumania, 90,000 Jews in Slovakia, 140,000 in Holland and 2 million in the Soviet Union. They also controlled the fate of the Jews of France, Belgium, Luxembourg, Italy, Norway, Greece and such remote places as the islands of Crete and Rhodes (see map, p. 150).

Thus, the two events, the Holocaust and World War II, converged *geographically*, but in all other respects should not be confused. For example, there were no military or political reasons to annihilate the Jews. In fact, it was a military burden for the Germans to take so many men and trains away from the war effort in order to carry out the "Final Solution."

The official position of each Allied government (Great Britain, France, the Soviet Union and the United States) was to offer assistance to active political and/or military opponents of the Germans. This must be understood in order to grasp the policy pursued by the Allies regarding the murder of the Jews.

- The Jews were not a nation.
- The Jews were not a political force or political party.
- The Jews were not a unified armed enemy of Germany.

Therefore, the Allies did not help rescue the Jews.

OUTLINE: THE SOUNDS OF SILENCE:
WORLD RESPONSES TO THE HOLOCAUST

I. **What the Allies Knew and How They Responded:**

    A. **The Newspapers:**

        1. **1938:**

            a.

            b.

        2. **1941:**

        3. **1942:**

            a.

                1)

                2)

                3)

            b.

                1)

                2)

                RESPONSE: **Denials:**

B. **Other Sources of Information:**

1. **World Jewish Congress:**

RESPONSE:

2. **U.S. Air Force:**

RESPONSE:

3. **Polish Underground:**

RESPONSE: a.

b.

1)

2)

3)

WHEN THE ALLIES REFUSED TO BOMB AUSCHWITZ IN 1944, THE NAZIS WERE KILLING 15,000 JEWS EACH DAY. ONE BOMB, DESTROYING ONE GAS CHAMBER OR ONE RAILROAD LINE, MIGHT HAVE SAVED THOUSANDS OF LIVES.

4. **Jan Karski:**

   a.

   b.

   RESPONSE:

ROOSEVELT INSISTED THAT THE WAR AND THE HOLOCAUST WERE THE SAME. TO HIM, FIGHTING THE GERMANS WAS AUTOMATICALLY HELPING THE JEWS. THIS OPINION ALLOWED THE HOLOCAUST TO CONTINUE AND RESULTED IN THE DEATHS OF HUNDREDS OF THOUSANDS OF INNOCENT PEOPLE.

5. **Roumanian Government:**

   RESPONSE:

6. **Bermuda Conference:**

   RESPONSE:

7. **Adolf Eichmann:**

RESPONSE:

8. **War Refugee Board:**

RESPONSE:

9. **Escaped Prisoners:**

RESPONSE:

a.

b.

c.

d.

e.

B. **Some Reasons for the Allied Responses:**

1. **War Propaganda:**

2. **Disbelief:**

3. **German Denials:**

4. **Anti-Semitism:**

5. **"Useless People":**

THE LAST REASON IS PERHAPS THE MOST DISTURBING BECAUSE IT SUGGESTS THAT THE MORALITY OF SOME ALLIED BUREAUCRATS WAS NOT UNLIKE THE MORALITY OF GERMAN BUREAUCRATS.

II. **What the Christian Churches Knew and How They Responded:**

A. **The Vatican:**

1. **The Pope:**

2. **The Concordat:**

a. **Papal Silence:**

b. Vatican Opposition to the Third Reich:

3. "Final Solution":

4. The Fate of Italian Jews:

a.

1)

2)

b.

c.

d. Papal Silence:

1)

2)

3)

5. **Rescue:**

VATICAN SOURCES ESTIMATE POPE PIUS XII WAS RESPONSIBLE FOR SECRETLY DIRECTING OR APPROVING CATHOLIC ASSISTANCE TO HUNDREDS OF THOUSANDS OF JEWS. HAD THE POPE MORE OPENLY AND OFFICIALLY CONDEMNED NAZI ACTIONS, MORE JEWS MIGHT HAVE BEEN SAVED.

6. **Some Reasons for the Vatican Responses:**

   a. **Fear of Reprisals:**

   b. **Fear for the Jews:**

   c. **Catholic Lands:**

   d. **Anti-Communism:**

B. **Individual Protests:**

   1. **German Catholic Opponents of Nazism:**

      a.

      b.

      c.

      d.

      e.

C. Some Protestant Responses to the Holocaust:

   1. Individuals:

      a. Andre Trocme:

      b. Archbishop Damskinos:

   2. The Confessing Church:

      a. Niemoeller and Barth:

      b. The Barmen Confession:

      c. Dietrich Bonhoeffer:

      d. Protestant Opponents of Nazism:

   3. Church Policy:

D. Some Reasons for the Protestant Responses:

   1. Danger:

   2. Religious Principles:

III. Summary

Shmuel Zygelboim wrote that the primary responsibility for the murder of the Jews was with the murderers themselves. But, what drove him to despair and suicide was the realization that the Allies, too, shared the responsibility by refusing to help when and where they could.

THE PRIMARY RESPONSIBILITY FOR THE MURDER OF THE JEWS LIES WITH THE PERPETRATORS, THE GERMAN DESTRUCTION MACHINE. BUT THE SECONDARY RESPONSIBILITY COMES FROM INDIFFERENCE AND REFUSAL TO ACT. THE ALLIES DID NOT DETERMINE "WHO SHALL LIVE AND WHO SHALL DIE," BUT THEY WERE INDIRECTLY INVOLVED IN SUCH DECISIONS. CHURCH OFFICIALS OF DIFFERENT CHRISTIAN DENOMINATIONS DID NOT CONTROL THOSE LIFE AND DEATH DECISIONS. YET, SOME OF THEM FAILED AS MORAL LEADERS OF THE CHRISTIAN WORLD.

Reading 16D

AFTERMATH AND LIBERATION

Question

What do you think are four of the main points in this reading?

In January 1945, the Russian forces, the Red Army, approached Auschwitz. The officials of I.G. Farben and the SS officers of Auschwitz burned records and dismantled Birkenau and Monowitz. By the time soldiers of the Red Army marched into Auschwitz, the Germans had fled. The Russians found 6,000 sick, emaciated prisoners in the "infirmary" of the main camp. Among them were almost 200 starving children.

The Third *Reich* seemed to be falling apart as the Allied troops closed in. On the Eastern Front, the Russian troops fed those survivors they found, then either drafted them into service or sent them to Russia. The Red Army was determined to reach Berlin and continued to move forward, taking little time to help the victims of the camps.

The same held true in the West: the war was still on and to many British and American units, the camps were a distraction from their main purpose. The troops that liberated Landsberg, a concentration and labor camp in Germany, for example, considered the inmates a "problem" and moved on within six days. Prisoners had to be "deloused" and their uniforms burned. They had to be issued new clothing. There was little time to treat the broken victims with proper sympathy.

In April and May 1945, American troops marched into German concentration camps. The Americans were greeted by blank stares from skeleton-like people. The stench and sight was enough to cause physical and mental disorders among the American troops. None of them had been told what they would find in the camps. Most had heard about concentration camps but had little idea that such horrors existed. They were shocked by what they discovered. One of the American soldiers who liberated the concentration camp at Landsberg recalls that "even at its least terrible, it was incredibly terrible . . . It simply boggles the mind . . . You have to not just see it; you have to smell it . . . There was a kind of shock. I think we were in a state of shock. We were unprepared for this . . . There was no cheering. They were just . . . they had given up . . . almost given up hope."

Bewildered, the troops had little choice but to begin to disinfect the Jews of the camps. Many who remembered the same orders to undress and be "deloused" when they had first arrived at the concentration camps were frightened.

Auschwitz had been "liquidated," that is, taken apart. Over 58,000 prisoners were forced to march in the bitter cold toward Germany. So began the Death Marches. No one was allowed to stop for any reason whatsoever unless the guards stopped the whole column for a brief rest period. Those who fell from exhaustion were shot. Those who stopped for some reason or stumbled were also shot. Small groups of prisoners were given wagons to push and were forced to pick up the dead bodies and put them on the wagons. When the wagons were full, they had to stop and bury the dead. One survivor remembers picking up a body and hearing his name called. The man was alive. "Let me carry him, he is still alive," said the survivor to the guard. The guard put the rifle to his head and forced him to bury the still living man.

The survivors of these Death Marches were herded into various camps in Germany, the worst being Bergen-Belsen. Tens of thousands arrived within a week. They were crammed into barracks and left to starve. Many of the Germans changed into civilian clothes and ran. Yet, a few guards remained, shooting any prisoners who had the strength to venture out of the barracks. To the very end, then, the "Final Solution" continued. Even as the perpetrators lost the war and ran from the Allies, they tried to finish the task of murdering the Jews.

When the British forces arrived at Bergen-Belsen, they found dead bodies rotting in the mud. Corpses were piled everywhere. The stench of the camp could be smelled for miles. Rats had begun to gnaw on the living, and some of the desperately starved people had begun to eat the flesh of the dead. When the storehouses were opened by the British, those survivors who were able stormed them and raced out with tin cans of food. Many dropped dead within minutes because of the inability to digest food of that type after years of malnourishment. The British then locked the storehouses, began disinfecting prisoners and carefully started to feed them. Many of the British soldiers had to be admitted to hospitals for psychological disorders after observing the horrible conditions.

Other inmates of smaller labor and concentration camps began to escape as the German system crumbled. Many ran into forests seeking refuge in German or Polish homes. Some found sympathetic responses, others were driven away or shot.

The Allies set up displaced persons camps (DP camps) as quickly as possible, and most of the survivors were placed into them. Some spent the next four years in one or more of these camps. Others immediately began thinking about going to the United States or Palestine. Still others returned home, seeking relatives or friends. Of those who tried to return home, many were attacked by native populations. In 1946, in Kielce {kels}, Poland, there was a pogrom. Over 40 Jews who had returned to this city were murdered. In smaller towns across Poland, Slovakia, and parts of Hungary, similar outrages took place.

Jews became more aware that they had lost their homes and had no country. As they returned to their former homes, they found no families left. Survivors tell of losing 50, 60, 70 or more members of their families. "Only then when I arrived back home did I wish I had not survived," said one survivor. "What was there to live for? My parents, my sisters and brother, all my aunts and uncles, cousins, friends, teachers--everyone was gone." Synagogues had been looted and burned. Whole communities had been destroyed--approximately 4,500 of them.

Continuity had been central to Jewish life and culture in Europe. That continuity gave Jews a feeling of things continuing from the past to the present and into the future, a feeling of certainty. That continuity had been broken. With the death of so many children, almost one and a half million, an entire generation had been destroyed. Almost no one over 35 had survived. Traditions that dated back 2,000 years had come to an end. With the loss of continuity, traditions and lives, European Jewish culture, a way of life, came to an end. In that respect, the "Final Solution" was a success.

Aftermath: Consequences and Implications

HOLOCAUST CURRICULUM

Aftermath:
Consequences and Implications

BRINGING THE PERPETRATORS TO JUSTICE

Questions

1. Do you think justice was achieved by the Nuremberg Trials? Should there have been other defendants?

2. Do you agree with Chief Justice Jackson's statement about not interfering in the laws and practices of other governments?

3. Should there have been a separate category for crimes committed against the Jews?

War Crimes

In 1943, the Allies began to prepare for military war crimes trials. Those trials were held in 1945 and 1946 in Nuremberg, one of Germany's oldest cities. The Nuremberg Trials were conducted by an International Military Tribunal made up of judges and prosecutors from the four Allied powers: France, Great Britain, the Soviet Union and the United States. The trials were approved by 19 other nations. As war crimes trials, they dealt with Nazi actions connected to aggression in war—attacking other nations—not specifically with crimes dealing with Jews or the Holocaust. Twenty-one German leaders were tried as war criminals. The first charge against them was "Conspiracy to Commit Aggressive War." Seven organizations were also accused of crimes: The *Reich* Cabinet, the Nazi Leadership Corps, the German General Staff, the *Gestapo*, the SD or Secret Service *(Sicherheitsdienst)*, the SS and the SA.

Chief Justice Jackson, the presiding American judge, stated:

> The way Germany treats its inhabitants, or any other country treats its inhabitants, is not our affair any more than it is the affair of some other government to interpose itself in our problems . . .

The Tribunal agreed, declaring that "the atrocities committed inside Germany, under German law . . . by authorities of the German state" were off limits. This included the anti-Jewish decrees and laws passed during the 1930s.

Germany had attacked other countries and broken the peace. German forces had killed civilians. These actions were among the war crimes. Jews were among the civilian populations of those countries—Poland, France, Holland, Belgium, Norway, the Soviet Union, Hungary, Roumania and others. The killing of Jews *as Jews* was not considered as a separate crime. Thus, a general who gave orders to attack Polish cities, to imprison and abuse Polish prisoners of war or murder Jewish and non-Jewish citizens as part of the attack, could be accused of committing war crimes.

The chief of the British prosecutors knew that the murder of the Jews had "shocked the conscience of our people" and would have to be considered in the lists of the crimes. But he would list "only such general treatment of the Jews as showed itself as part of the general plan of aggression."

Crimes Against Humanity

The Allies recognized that atrocities—extremely evil, cruel or inhuman acts—had been committed against whole populations. The term "crimes against humanity" was created by the International Tribunal. These crimes were to include "enslavement and mass murder." "War crimes" dealt with violence against countries and governments. "Crimes against humanity" dealt with violence done to civilian populations, citizens of those countries. In practice, "crimes against humanity" were limited to acts of aggression committed against national civilian populations: the Poles, Hungarians, French, etc. The killing of Jews because they were Jews was not listed as a crime.

Only one defendant, Julius Streicher, was condemned solely on the basis of his guilt for "crimes against humanity." He had little or nothing to do with the war, but his newspaper was the most vicious anti-Jewish and racist Nazi publication. He was second to none—not even Hitler—in his anti-Jewish ravings. Recognizing this unusual position, the International Tribunal sentenced him to death only on the basis of "crimes against humanity."

Only top-ranking Nazi or German officials were accused of crimes. Those condemned to death were executed because of their role in World War II. Highest ranking among them was Hermann Goering, Deputy Chancellor to Hitler. He committed suicide in his cell after his trial. Heinrich Himmler, who had been next highest, never got to trial. He committed suicide after being captured by the American Army. (Hitler had committed suicide in his underground bunker in Berlin.) (See Appendix C, p. 200 "List of Major Nazi Leaders," for the fates of other Nazi leaders.)

The thousands of low-ranking officials involved in war crimes or crimes against humanity were ignored or received light sentences and many resumed their careers.

The murder of Jews at Auschwitz, Treblinka and the other death camps, and the killings by the *Einsatzgruppen,* were not issues beyond their involvement with the German war effort. Although some organizations like the *Gestapo* were involved in mass murder, it could not be shown that they waged war. In the end, membership in those organizations did not count as a crime—even if it meant being a part of the concentration and death camp system. As one historian has noted, the phrase "'crimes against humanity' became deadwood," that is, an empty phrase that had no real meaning in the trials. There were no penalties for the killing of Jews as Jews.

Other trials were conducted at Nuremberg until 1949. Approximately 185 leading Nazi and German officials were tried. These included two leaders of the *Einsatzgruppen,* both of whom were executed, several doctors, industrialists like I. G. Farben officials, and leaders in the Nazi organizations. A small proportion of these officials were executed; some were given life sentences in prison; most were given lesser prison sentences.

After 1953, trials of Nazis were not confined only to war-related activities and were conducted in other countries by national governments. France conducted trials against Nazis who had committed crimes against French citizens, Poland conducted trials on behalf of Polish citizens, etc. In 1961, the first trial to deal solely with crimes against Jews or Holocaust-related actions took place in Jerusalem. Adolf Eichmann had been caught in Argentina by Israeli secret service agents. He was brought to Jerusalem where he was tried for crimes committed against the Jewish people and crimes against humanity. After a lengthy trial, he was found guilty and hanged.

L E S S O N 18

Aftermath: Consequences and Implications

174

Reading 18A

IMPLICATIONS OF THE HOLOCAUST

The authors of this unit on the Holocaust think that each of the following implications of the Holocaust must be considered as lessons to be learned for the present and the future. It is their belief that these implications, taken from careful examination of the experiences of the victims and the actions of the perpetrators, have profound consequences for our lives today.

"Ask not for whom the bell tolls—it tolls for thee."

John Donne

CONSEQUENCES OF:

TOLERANCE OF PERSECUTION:

Because of opportunities to advance careers or social status, or to gain profits, average citizens might neglect ethics and allow discrimination and persecution to go on.

DEHUMANIZATION:

Dehumanization of any person or group, turning people into objects, seems necessary for a tragic event like the Holocaust to occur. During the Holocaust, Jews were no longer perceived as humans, but as a problem or "question" that needed an efficient solution.

QUESTION OF CONSCIENCE:

As a guide for proper behavior, conscience might become an inconvenience and be replaced by ideology, profit, silence, science or social status. SS leaders recognized that the established moral codes could not exist if their goal, to destroy all Jews, was to be reached.

PERSONAL RESPONSIBILITY:

It is the responsibility of human beings to *think*—especially about the consequences of their actions. Those who do not think beyond their immediate tasks or consider the consequences of their actions still share the responsibility for what happens around them.

All those involved in the killing process—railroad employees, chemists, doctors, civil servants, lawyers, clergymen, physicists, engineers, craftsmen, architects, businessmen, plumbers, university professors, accountants—stopped thinking beyond their immediate tasks. The chemists producing Zyklon B never thought beyond the production in their laboratories. The doctors performing experiments never thought beyond the "scientific" and racial rationalizations. Railroad officials never thought beyond getting cattle cars full of people to their destinations quickly and efficiently.

All these people shared the guilt of the killers.

ABUSE OF TECHNOLOGY:

Science and technology, logic and efficiency are potential tools for evil when used by an unethical government. The great advances in science and technology, and in methods of organization and efficiency easily served the forces of destruction of human life. Technological progress was not moral progress.

INDIFFERENCE:

Personal responsibility extends beyond one's immediate surroundings to the suffering of others. The Allies shared in the responsibility for the murder of the Jews because of their indifference, apathy and/or refusal to help rescue the victims.

PERSONAL COURAGE:

Perhaps the most important implication or lesson comes from the examples of the rescuers. In spite of pressures, non-Jews all over Europe refused to collaborate in the "Final Solution." These individuals chose to act according to a standard of behavior, a code of ethics, that put human life ahead of other considerations. As one scholar wrote, referring to the rescue of the Jews in Denmark, the history of the Holocaust shows us that "it could happen in most places but it did not happen everywhere."

LIFE WORTHY OF LIFE:

The idea of "useless people" or of "surplus populations" is one that threatens everyone. On that basis, millions of innocent victims were murdered. On that basis, where human dignity or the sanctity of life are rejected, mass murder is a continuing danger.

"Our only hope will lie in the frail web of understanding
of one person for the pain of another."

John Dos Passos (1940)

APPENDICES

GLOSSARY OF KEY TERMS

Alienation: Feelings of separation from others or from meaningful activity; confusion about life and the future.

Allies: The four major opponents of Germany in World War II: France, Great Britain, the Soviet Union and the United States.

Anti-Semitism: Prejudice against Jews; dislike of Jews; discrimination or persecution of Jews.

Appel: Roll call in the camps.

Appelplatz: Roll call area in concentration, labor and death camps.

Armistice: Peace; calling a halt to armed hostilities.

Aryan: Has no biological validity as a racial term. Used by the Nazis to mean a superior, white, Nordic heroic type.

Auschwitz: City in Southwestern Poland near Kracow near which the most famous and largest concentration and death camps were located. By the end of 1942, Auschwitz was the center of the "Final Solution."

Beer-hall Putsch: The event that took place in Munich, Germany, in 1923 when Hitler led an attempt to seize the government (a *putsch*). The putsch failed and resulted in a jail sentence for him and a lesson that in order to gain power he would have to work within the system.

Belzec: Death camp located in Poland. Jews were murdered in gas chambers as carbon monoxide gas from an engine was pumped in. An estimated 500,000 Jews were killed there.

Bergen-Belsen: Concentration camp in Germany. After the death and labor camps in the East were taken apart, thousands of the emaciated prisoners were forced into Bergen-Belsen.

Bermuda Conference on Refugees: Anglo-American Conference held in Bermuda, April 1943, to decide what to do about those in flight from the Nazis, especially Jews. The conference produced no plan and revealed the indifference of Allied governments.

Birkenau: Auschwitz II, the death camp and site of the four gas chambers in which Jews and others were killed.

Brezhinka: The storehouse of clothing collected from the victims at Auschwitz. The mountain of clothing was sorted by prisoners for suitable things to send back to Germany.

Buchenwald: One of the first concentration camps in Germany. Located near Weimar, the cultural capital of 18th and 19th century Germany, it was built around the "Goethe Oak," the tree beneath which the great German Enlightenment poet, Wolfgang Goethe, sat and wrote.

Bund: Jewish political organization in Poland which was represented in the Polish parliament.

Castration: Surgical removal of the testicles or genitals.

Chelmno: The first death camp, located in Poland, constructed in 1941 for the purpose of murdering Jews. The victims of Chelmno died in gas vans and were buried in mass graves. An estimated 100,000 Jews were murdered there.

Collective Responsibility: The act of holding a group responsible for the actions of any of its individual members.

Concentration Camp: Place in which prisoners of the state are kept. In Germany, concentration camps began as an instrument of intimidation for political opponents of the Nazis and because the prisons were full. Later, they became a standing weapon of terror. Ultimately, over 100 camps were set up where people were "concentrated," that is, kept in one place. While they were related to the labor and death camps, they were not the same. Probably millions of people died in the concentration camps, but they were not set up as death camps like Treblinka, Sobibor and Auschwitz II (Birkenau). Auschwitz I was the concentration camp of the Auschwitz complex.

Crematorium: Ovens or furnaces where concentration and death camp prisoners' bodies were burned.

Dachau: The first concentration camp opened by the Nazis in 1933 near Munich, Germany. It served as a camp to concentrate political opponents of the Third Reich, democratic supporters of the Weimar Republic, Socialists, Communists and others who were mainly non-Jews.

Death Camps: These camps were Nazi centers of murder or extermination. Jews and non-Jews were brought to them to be put to death as part of Hitler's "Final Solution." The six death camps (Auschwitz, Treblinka, Sobibor, Maidanek, Chelmno and Belzec) were established solely for the murder of Europe's Jews. Eventually, had the war continued, they would have been used to annihilate other groups the Nazis considered inferior, like the Poles. The death camps, especially Auschwitz, were also the places of death for nearly a half million Gypsies.

Death Marches:	The prisoners of Auschwitz and other camps in Poland were forced by the Germans to march to camps in Germany as the Russian armies approached from the east. The death camps were taken apart and the prisoners were forced onto the roads in the bitter January cold of 1945. About one third of the prisoners died on the death marches.
Deportation:	Term used for the forced removal of Jews in Nazi occupied lands under the pretense of "resettlement." Most Jews were shipped to the death camps.
Displaced Persons:	Term used to refer to those survivors of the Holocaust who had no homes after the war and were often placed in Displaced Persons Camps.
Displaced Persons Camps:	Camps opened by the Allies after the war to temporarily house the refugees of Europe.
Dolchstosslegende:	The myth of the "stab in the back" used by the Nazis and other opponents of the democratic Weimar Republic. These people claimed that Germany had lost World War I because the Jews and Communists had plotted against Germany from within.
Dysentery:	An infectious disease which produces diarrhea which becomes uncontrollable and often leads to internal bleeding and ulcer and stomach complications. The ghettos and camps were constantly battling the infection of dysentery.
Einsatzgruppen:	SS mobile killing units, attached to the German Army, whose primary purpose was to seek out and slaughter Jews in Eastern Poland and Russia.
Euthanasia:	The policy of so-called "mercy-killing" which the Nazi government passed into law in 1933. Their plans were to kill the "feeble-minded," old, physically handicapped or "useless" people in Germany. The "Euthanasia Program" became the foundation for the planning of the "Final Solution." The plans for killing the Jews included practices similar to those used in the "Euthanasia Program." The "Final Solution" also used many of the same staff.
Extermination:	Term used to refer to the annihilation or total destruction of the Jews. Extermination calls up images of pests or non-human creatures to be killed by use of pesticides.
Extermination Camps:	Six camps established in Poland for the purpose of killing Jews—Auschwitz, Treblinka, Sobibor, Maidanek, Chelmno and Belzec.

Fascism:	An extreme conservative political philosophy, usually ultra-nationalistic, violent, anti-Communist, anti-Semitic or racist. German fascism was National Socialism or Nazism.
Final Solution:	The Nazi term for their program to annihilate the Jews of Europe. A euphemism or substitute term for mass murder or genocide. The term refers to the last in a line of "solutions" to the "problem" of what to do with the Jews.
Freikorps:	Bands of armed fighters who roamed the streets of Germany in the 1920s as violent defenders of right-wing political ideas and parties. The Nazi SA was formed from one of these groups.
Fuehrer:	German word for leader. Hitler was called the *Fuehrer*, meaning the supreme leader of his people. The term implies great prestige and power.
Gas Chamber:	Buildings or parts of buildings which were sealed off and air-tight so that large numbers of people could be murdered by poison gas which was released into the chamber. The primary method of murder used in the death camps.
Generalkomissar:	Nazi SS commander of an occupied region.
Genocide:	The systematic killing of a whole people or nation.
Gestapo:	Abbreviation for *Geheimnis Staats Polizei* or Secret State Police. The *Gestapo* was a branch of the SS which dealt with political opponents with terror and arbitrary arrest. In 1939, the *Gestapo* took control of Jewish emigration, which meant it was in charge of expelling Jews from all German-controlled areas.
Ghetto:	The section of a city in which Jews were required to live. Ghettos were established in cities with railroad connections. The ghettos were sometimes surrounded by guards, barbed wire or brick walls. If Jews were found outside the ghetto without special permission they were killed.
Paul Joseph Goebbels:	Nazi in charge of propaganda. He was a master of mass media techniques. His speech on the night of November 9, 1938, touched off the *Kristallnacht.*
Hermann Goering:	Deputy Chancellor to Hitler, also in charge of the air force and gave the order to Heydrich to begin the "Final Solution."

Wolfgang Goethe: Most famous 18th century German Enlightenment poet and philosopher who represented tolerance, reason, international peace and the great ideas of the time. He was the model German for German Jews.

Gypsies: A group designated by the Nazis as "parasites" and criminals. The Criminal Police and the SS were instructed to arrest any persons who "looked like" Gypsies or were wanderers in a "Gypsie-like" manner. There were some racial theorists who thought Gypsies were somehow of the same "race" as Jews. Most of the Nazi officials saw them as criminal rather than racial enemies. A series of laws like the Nuremberg Laws was drafted for Gypsies. It is estimated that over 250,000 Gypsies were murdered by the Nazis, many of those at Auschwitz.

Reinhard Heydrich: Head of the Main Office of the SS; he coordinated the many departments necessary to carry out the "Final Solution." Heydrich was a brilliant organizer and vicious anti-Semite. He was Heinrich Himmler's assistant.

Heinrich Himmler: Head of the SS. He was responsible only to Hitler and gave the orders for the annihilation of the Jews. He was a careful organizer of details and devoted to Hitler. Directly responsible for the "Final Solution."

Hippocratic Oath: The oath taken by all doctors in which they swear to heal the sick and not harm any human beings.

Holocaust: The term which refers to the systematic murder of approximately six million Jews between 1933 and 1945. The word is a Greek translation of a word used in the Book of Genesis in the *Bible* which means "total burning" and refers to a sacrifice to God.

I. G. Farben: German industrial trust which was the largest chemical conglomerate, controlling company, in Europe. It included corporations like BASF, German Bayer, and numerous others. I. G. Farben used Jewish slave laborers from concentration and labor camps, financed medical experiments, and even constructed its own labor camp at Auschwitz (Auschwitz III, Monowitz) where the largest synthetic rubber factory in the world was being built.

Jewish Question: The term refers to the anti-Semitic question of "what to do with the Jews." The policies followed under the Nazis included three answers: separation from the rest of German society, expulsion and, finally, annihilation—the "Final Solution to the Jewish Question."

Juden: German word for Jews.

Judenrat: Jewish Council: administrative organizations set up in each ghetto by the German occupation forces to organize and administer the ghettos.

Judenrein: German term meaning "pure" or "clean" of Jews. The goal of the Nazi "Final Solution" or the Holocaust.

Kapo: Abbreviation for *Kameraden Polizei* or "Comrade Police." Kapos were prisoners, Jewish and non-Jewish, who were selected by German guards to oversee labor details or their barracks in the concentration and labor camps. They frequently became as violent or more violent than the Germans. Had they acted less violently, they would have been murdered, too.

Kristallnacht: "Night of the broken glass." Using the shooting of a minor German official in Paris, Ernst vom Rath, by a young Jewish student, the Nazis, organized and led by SA men all over Germany, carried out three nights of violence against Jews, Jewish homes, synagogues and businesses. The Nazis smashed, burned and looted. Over 35,000 Jews were arrested and taken into "Protective Custody" and sent to concentration camps for days or weeks; many were beaten in the streets; about 35 were killed. This was the last pogrom in Germany, and it took place on November 9-11, 1938. Among the results were the enormous claims filed by Germans against German insurance companies; openly hostile publicity from foreign reporters who observed the anti-Jewish riots; protests from foreign ministries—including the United States. President Roosevelt temporarily withdrew the American Ambassador to Germany. The Jews were charged a billion mark penalty to pay for the damages and the event was followed by a series of anti-Jewish laws.

Labor Camp: A camp whose prisoners were used for slave labor by German businesses, SS, the government or the military.

Landsberg: A labor camp in Germany which was liberated by the American forces in 1945. It became a Displaced Persons Camp.

Lebensraum: German word for "living space." Hitler's goal in the war was to gain *Lebensraum* for Germans in the East. This meant enslaving or killing the native populations of Poland and other Eastern European countries.

Left-wing (political): Political groups or individuals that were liberal in their outlook. This usually meant democratic, advocating equal rights for all citizens, tolerance and peace between nations.

Gotthold Lessing: An 18th century German Enlightenment philosopher and writer who championed reason, tolerance, equal rights and peace. He wrote a famous play about a wise Jew called "Nathan the Wise" which became famous in Germany. He was a close friend of Moses Mendelssohn, the German Jewish philosopher.

Maidanek: Death and concentration camp in Poland where an estimated 200,000 Jews and 30,000 Polish non-Jews were killed in gas chambers.

Mauthausen: Concentration and labor camp located in Austria. Although not designated as a death camp, hundreds of thousands of Jews and non-Jews were killed there in the Nazi program of "extermination through labor."

Moses Mendelssohn: An 18th century German Enlightenment philosopher and writer and close friend of the famous Gotthold Lessing. He became known as "the first German Jew" because he assumed the role of both German and Jew by writing in German, dressing like the Germans and discussing German issues. Yet, he maintained his Jewish identity as well. This attitude was known as assimilation and served as a model for German Jews who came after him.

Monowitz: The I. G. Farben labor camp at Auschwitz (Auschwitz III).

Nationalism: Devotion to one's nation; excessive patriotism; the doctrine that national interests are more important than anything else.

National Socialism: The political and social philosophy of Hitler and of Germany from 1933-1945. National Socialism meant dictatorship and included the philosophy of racism as its rationale. German fascism was called National Socialism.

National Socialist Bond: Dutch Nazi Party.

Nazi: Abbreviation for National Socialist German Workers Party (NSDAP).

Nazi Party: Abbreviation for National Socialist German Workers Party (NSDAP).

Nazi-Soviet Pact: The agreement between the Soviet Union and Germany signed on August 30, 1939. The two countries agreed to divide Poland when Germany conquered it and also agreed to remain neutral should either be involved in a war.

Nazism: Abbreviation for National Socialism, the political philosophy and system of government under Hitler in Germany from 1933-1945. In practice, it meant dictatorship or total control by Hitler.

Nuremberg Laws:	In 1935, Hitler made anti-Semitism part of Germany's legal code. These laws defined Jews, excluded Jews from German society, and removed all their civil rights.
Nuremberg Trials:	Trials conducted after World War II by an International Military Tribunal set up by the Allies. High ranking Nazi leaders were charged with War Crimes and "Crimes Against Humanity." Twenty-one were charged; 19 were convicted; 12 received the death penalty.
Partisan:	Native guerilla-type fighters who resisted the Nazi invasion after their countries were defeated.
Perpetrator:	A participant in the killing of the Jews. This term includes all those who were involved even from far away: bureaucrats, lawyers, architects, chemists, businessmen, railroad officials, diplomats, etc.
Pogrom:	An attack on Jews by mobs of non-Jews. These attacks were violent, including rape, murder and the looting and destruction of Jewish property. Jews suffered from pogroms for centuries. Whole communities were violently and viciously destroyed. Pogroms usually lasted for a short time—hours to days—and then were over. Jews would return and begin again. Pogroms were not systematic, organized or continuous; they were not what historian Raul Hilberg has called a "destruction process" which is carried out administratively and continues until it achieves its final goal: in this case, the annihilation of the Jews. The Holocaust was not the same as a pogrom.
Pope:	The spiritual leader of the Roman Catholic Church; also the Bishop of Rome and the political authority of Vatican City.
Protocols of the Elders of Zion:	An anti-Semitic book written near the end of the 19th century. It was a proven forgery which claimed that there was an international Jewish conspiracy to take over the world and destroy "pure" "Aryan" Christian civilization. The book was financed in the U.S. by Henry Ford. It was one of the best selling books in Europe in the 1920s.
Propaganda:	The systematic spreading of particular ideas, doctrines or policies, usually through the mass media, to advance a particular cause or person.
Racism:	A philosophy or program of discrimination, segregation, persecution based on the idea of one race being superior to others. Modern scientists consider the concept of "race" to be a false one. The Nazis considered the "Aryan Race," Germanic and Christian, to be destined to rule the world because of its "blood superiority." They considered Jews a race of inferior and undesirable sub-humans. They had similar views of Gypsies, Poles, Blacks and Slavs.

Ravensbruck: A concentration camp located in Germany. It held only women prisoners.

Red Army: The army of the Soviet Union.

Refugee: Someone who has lost or been driven from his/her home and is homeless.

Reich: German word for empire.

Reichsfuehrer SS: Commander-in-Chief of the SS; Heinrich Himmler's title.

Reichstag: The German parliament or legislating body.

Reparations: Payments made by Germany to the Allies (Great Britain, France and the United States) after World War I.

Right-wing (political): Individuals or political parties that were nationalistic, conservative, usually anti-democratic. In Germany, these groups were often connected with anti-Semitic tendencies.

SA: Abbreviation for *Sturm Abteilung*, the Storm Section or Storm Troopers. The SA were the brown-shirted units organized to protect the early Nazi meetings and terrorize those who opposed Hitler. Their membership grew to 400,000 by 1930. They were known as the violent street fighters of the Nazi Party. Hitler had hundreds of the SA leadership murdered in June 1934 because they were hurting his prestige as Chancellor of Germany with their ineffective and crude violence. The SS was originally a part of the SA but was separated from it in 1936.

Scapegoat: A person or group who is the object of hatred and even violence in a situation where prejudiced people must place blame for their mistakes or actions on others.

Selection: The procedure to determine who would live and who would die at death and labor camps. The most famous of these was Auschwitz. The selections were usually carried out or directed by medical doctors who were considered professionally qualified to make the decisions.

SD: Abbreviation for the Security Police *(Sicherheitsdienst)*, the branch of the SS that was the secret service with the job of protecting national security. The SD was involved with with running the death camps and was the branch of the SS that contained the *Einsatzgruppen,* or mobile killing units.

SS:	Abbreviation for *Schutzstaffel* or protection squads. Originally a part of the SA, they were picked as the elite guard to watch over Hitler. Their numbers grew from 200 to 4 million by 1940. Headed by Heinrich Himmler, they became known as the most efficient organization in the Third *Reich*. Eventually, the enormous SS bureaucracy was like a state within a state. It controlled the concentration, labor and death camps. It included an armed section who fought as crack troops in the war, a secret service unit, the *Gestapo* or secret police; and it controlled almost every aspect of the "Final Solution." SS men were trained to hate all "enemies of the Reich," especially Jews.
Sobibor:	Death camp in Poland. An estimated 250,000 Jews died there in gas chambers. In 1943 Sobibor was blown up by prisoners who then escaped. Most were caught and killed.
Sonderkommando:	Special units of prisoners given the duty of transporting bodies from the gas chambers to the crematoria and cleaning out the crematoria ovens. Each unit lasted a few months and was then killed.
Special Treatment (Besonderhandlung):	The term used in the concentration and death camps as a euphemism, a substitute word which hides the real meaning, for killing. "Special Treatment" meant gassing.
Josef Stalin:	Leader of the Soviet Union from 1924-1953. He signed the infamous Nazi-Soviet Pact with Hitler in August 1939 which made the invasion of Poland possible. After the German invasion of the Soviet Union in June 1941, Stalin led his people to victory as one of the Allied powers in World War II.
Stereotype:	A fixed image or idea of a person or group. Stereotypes place characteristics observed in a few members of a group onto the whole group.
Sudetenland:	Western Czechoslovakia which was given to Germany in 1938 without consulting with the Czech government. England and France, with the help of Italy, negotiated the agreement with Hitler. Within months of this, Hitler had his army move into the rest of Czechoslovakia.
Swastika:	An ancient symbol often used in Eastern religions as a symbol of life. In 1920, it was taken by the Nazi Party as its symbol. A twisted cross, it came to represent all the evils of Nazism.

Theresienstadt:	Concentration camp established in Czechoslovakia as a "model camp" to be shown to outside visitors from neutral countries like Switzerland or Sweden or members of the Red Cross. Almost all the Jews who were sent there, including thousands of children, were sent to Auschwitz and killed.
Third Reich:	The Third Empire; Hitler's name for his Germany and its administration from 1933-1945. The term comes from the First Empire of the Roman emperors, the Second of German Chancellor Bismarck in the 19th century, and the Third, Hitler's. Hitler thus saw himself as in the tradition of the Roman conquerors of Europe.
Treaty of Versailles:	One of the treaties signed to end World War I. The Versailles Treaty stripped Germany of much land, forced the government to pay reparations to the Allies and accused Germany of responsibility for World War I.
Treblinka:	Death camp in Poland. In its one year of existence an estimated 850,000 Jews were murdered there in gas chambers. In 1943, the camp was blown up in an uprising by the remaining 600 prisoners. All but 40 were killed.
Tuberculosis:	An infectious disease which usually attacks the lungs.
Typhus:	A severely infectious disease which brings a high fever, exhaustion and often death. The disease is carried by lice or fleas and was an uncontrollable killer in ghettos and in camps.
Uebermenschen:	Nazi term for "supermen" which to them was a racial idea. They hoped to create a race of biologically "pure" supermen.
Underground:	The secret groups fighting the Nazi occupation. The term includes the resistance movements in each country under Nazi rule during World War II.
Vatican:	The central authority for the Catholic Church; the authority and government of the pope. "Vatican" also refers to the residence of the pope in Vatican City.
Volk:	German word for "people" or nation. The term has a strongly nationalistic and even racial implication.
Volksgemeinschaft:	German word meaning "national community." It implies a family-like unity and some genetic bond between its members that is almost mystical.

War Refugee Board: Agency established by President Roosevelt in 1944 after much urging by Secretary of the Treasury Henry Morgenthau and members of the Treasury Department. It was established to negotiate the relief or rescue of war refugees, especially Jews.

Wehrmacht: The German Army (as distinguished from the SS).

Weimar Republic: The German government from 1919-1934. Its constitution was drafted in the city of Weimar, the poet Wolfgang Goethe's home and the 18th century cultural capital of Germany. The Republic's political center was in Berlin. A democratic republic like the United States, it was burdened with the aftermath of World War I, terrible inflation, violent enemies within like the Nazi Party, and an army that was not committed to defending a democracy. When Hitler combined the offices of Chancellor and President, in August 1934, the Weimar Republic came to an end.

World Jewish Congress: Agency founded to coordinate different Jewish organizations. During the war, it worked to help the Jews of Europe from its offices in Switzerland.

Yom Kippur: The Jewish Day of Atonement; the holiest day of the year for Jews on which they traditionally fast for 24 hours.

Zegota: Polish group connected to the underground resistance movement against the Nazis. Led by Colonel Henryk Wolinski and Adolf Berman, this group devoted itself to the rescue of Jews in Warsaw and Kracow. They managed to save 4,000-6,000 Jews.

Zyklon B: The cyanide gas made of prussic acid which was used to kill Jews in the gas chambers of Auschwitz. (The other death camps used carbon monoxide gas.) The gas was produced by a company called DEGESCH that was partly owned by I. G. Farben.

CHRONOLOGY OF EVENTS

Date	Event
January 30, 1933	Adolf Hitler is appointed Chancellor of the German *Reich*. He is the *Fuehrer* of the National Socialist, or Nazi, Party.
March 1933	Establishment of the first concentration camp in Germany near the small town of Dachau, outside Munich.
March 23, 1933	Convinced by Hitler that there is a state of emergency and a threat of Communist revolution, the *Reichstag* gives him the power to enact laws on his own.
April 1933	Anti-Jewish laws begin to be passed: Kosher butchering is forbidden; a quota for "non-Aryans" in schools is passed; "non-Aryan," that is, Jewish, civil servants are dismissed; Jews cannot become lawyers; quotas for Jews are passed in universities.
May 10, 1933	There are public burnings of books by Jewish authors and authors opposed to Nazi ideas. These include Helen Keller, Jack London, H.G. Wells, Thomas Mann, Dorothy Sanger and many others.
July 1933	Pope Pius XI signs a Concordat with Hitler.
July 14, 1933	The Nazi Party is proclaimed by law to be the one and only legal political party in Germany. Any people holding non-Nazi political meetings are subject to arrests and imprisonment in a concentration camp.

Date	Event
August 3, 1934	With the death of President von Hindenburg, Hitler declares himself president *and* chancellor—*Fuehrer* of the Third *Reich*.
September 15, 1935	Basic anti-Jewish laws are passed at Nuremberg (the Nuremberg Laws). These laws took German citizenship from Jews, removed their civil rights, reduced them to the status of "subjects," forbade marriage or any sexual relations between Jews and non-Jews; forbade Jews to employ non-Jewish women under age 45.
July 16, 1937	Buchenwald concentration camp opens near Weimar, Germany.
March 11-13, 1938	German troops march into Austria and Austria becomes part of the Third *Reich*. Five-hundred thousand people line the streets of Vienna to cheer Hitler as he is welcomed in Austria.
September 29-30, 1938	Munich Conference, attended by the heads of state of Great Britain (Chamberlain), France (Daladier), Italy (Mussolini) and Hitler. Britain and France agree to Germany's taking (annexing) part of Czechoslovakia. No Czech representative was present.
October 5, 1938	Jewish passports are marked with a "J" at the request of the Swiss government. The Swiss do not want German Jewish refugees.
October 28, 1938	Approximately 17,000 "stateless" Jews are deported from Germany to Poland.

Date	Event
November 7, 1938	After hearing of his parents' deportation, a young Jewish student, Herschel Grynszpan, shoots a German official in Paris.
November 9, 1938	The German official dies. Paul Goebbels, Nazi Minister of Propaganda, delivers a speech attacking Jews for "killing Germans." He has already issued instructions to the SA all across Germany to begin "spontaneous demonstrations" against the Jews. The result was the *Kristallnacht,* the "Night of the Broken Glass." German Jews were beaten in the streets, their homes and businesses were smashed, synagogues were looted and burned, and over 30,000 Jews were put in concentration camps for "protective custody."
November 12, 1938	Because of the insurance claims of non-Jews, the Jewish communities in Germany are forced to pay a one billion *Reichsmark* penalty to the German government.
November 15, 1938	All Jewish children remaining in German schools are removed to Jewish schools.
November 23, 1938	All Jewish businesses are closed down. Jewish doctors and pharmacists can only serve Jewish patients.
December 1938	Jews have been removed from businesses and schools; they are forbidden from certain neighborhoods; their bank accounts are seized by the government; they are forbidden from public museums, theaters, parks, baths, movies; their drivers' licenses are revoked; radios and telephones are removed.

Date	Event
March 15, 1939	German troops seize the rest of Czechoslovakia. Great Britain and France refuse to come to Czechoslovakia's aid. Independent Czechoslovakia disappears.
August 30, 1939	Germany and the Soviet Union sign the Nazi-Soviet Pact. Each country agrees to remain neutral if the other is engaged in a war.
September 1, 1939	Germany invades Poland.
September 3, 1939	Britain and France declare war on Germany as World War II begins.
September 17, 1939	The Red Army (Soviet Union) invades Eastern Poland. The secret clause of the Nazi-Soviet Pact becomes public. Independent Poland disappears.
October 12, 1939	Poland falls. The Nazi General Government is established as the Third *Reich* incorporates, or annexes, Western Poland.
November 23, 1939	Polish Jews must wear armbands with yellow Stars of David whenever they are on the streets.
November 28, 1939	Hans Frank, Governor General of occupied Poland, orders the forming of Jewish Councils in major cities. The first ghetto is set up in Piotrkow, Poland.
February 12, 1940	The *Gestapo* begin to take German Jews into "protective custody," that is, deport them to concentration camps.
April 9, 1940	German armies occupy Denmark and Southern Norway.
April 27, 1940	Himmler orders a concentration camp set up at Auschwitz, Poland.

Date	Event
May 10, 1940	Germany invades Holland, Belgium and France.
May 14, 1940	Holland surrenders.
June 29, 1940	France surrenders.
August 1940-December 1941	Anti-Jewish laws are passed in France, Roumania, Hungary, Italy, Poland and Holland.
November 15, 1940	Warsaw ghetto is sealed by a brick wall, which the Jews are forced to build.
April 6, 1941	German Army invades Greece and Yugoslavia.
June 22, 1941	Germany invades Eastern Poland, declaring war on the Soviet Union.
June 25, 1941	*Einsatzgruppen* begin their first *"Aktion,"* that is, attack on Jews, in Kaunas, Lithuania. The *Einsatzgruppen* continued their killing behind the German armies until December 1942. Using guns and gas vans, they murdered an estimated 1.4 million Jews.
July 31, 1941	Goering gives Heydrich a free hand in completing the "Final Solution."
September 1, 1941	All German Jews must wear a Star of David.
October 10, 1941	A "model ghetto" and concentration camp is established for "privileged Jews" in Theresienstadt, Czechoslovakia.
October 14, 1941	Mass deportations of Jews from all over Europe to concentration camps begins.
December 7, 1941	Japanese attack Pearl Harbor and the U.S. declares war on Japan.

Date	Event
December 11, 1941	Germany declares war on the U.S.
December 1941	Armed Jewish resistance groups begin to form around Minsk, Russia, and in France.
January 10, 1942	Jews in Germany must give up any woolen or fur clothing.
January 20, 1942	Heydrich convenes the Wanssee Conference in a suburb (Wanssee) of Berlin. Officials from the SS, the civil service, the diplomatic service, the railroads and the military are present. The subject is the details and methods to be used in carrying out the "Final Solution."
January 21, 1942	"Unified Partisan Organization" (FPO) established in the Vilna, Lithuania, ghetto.
March 1, 1942	Murder of the Jews at Sobibor, Poland, begins. By October 1943, when the camp was destroyed by the remaining prisoners, 250,000 Jews had been killed there.
1942	Increasingly harsh anti-Jewish laws are passed in Germany: Jews are forbidden telephones, radios, cigarettes, typewriters, bicycles, electrical and optical equipment and pets. They are banned from barber shops; Jewish schools are closed; Jews must give up all "spare" clothing.
June 1, 1942	Jews from Warsaw are shipped to the new death camp, Treblinka. By the time the camp is destroyed by the remaining 600 prisoners in August 1943, over 800,000 Jews had been killed there.

Date	Event
July 22, 1942	Germans order that 6,000-10,000 Jews a day be deported from Warsaw. The trains go to Treblinka. Adam Czerniakow, head of the Jewish Council of the Warsaw ghetto, commits suicide as the children of the orphanage are sent. By September 13, 1942, 300,000 Jews had been sent to Treblinka from Warsaw.
July 28, 1942	"Jewish Fighting Organization" (ZOB) is formed in the Warsaw ghetto.
1942	*Aktionen*, "actions," take place all over Europe. Millions of Jews are murdered by *Einsatzgruppen* or sent to the six death camps. Disease is widespread in all the ghettos; 500,000 Jews die between 1940 and 1944 in ghettos. Germans begin a policy of starvation of the Jews in Eastern Europe by keeping food from the ghettos. Mass murders occur regularly throughout Eastern Poland and the Soviet Union.
April 19, 1943	Bermuda Conference on Refugees. British and American officials discuss the possibilities of rescue of Europe's refugees, mainly Jews. Although they announce that secret plans are under way, they decide to do nothing.
	Warsaw Ghetto Rebellion begins, led by Mordechai Anielewicz and the ZOB.
May 16, 1943	Warsaw ghetto is burned to the ground; 55,000 Jews are captured and killed or sent to death or labor camps.
1942-1943	Jewish armed resistance in many ghettos: Czestachowa, Vilna, Bialystok, Tuchin, Minsk and others.
	Jewish prisoners revolt in Sobibor and Treblinka death camps. The camps are destroyed but only 40 of 600 escape at Treblinka and approximately 300 escape from Sobibor. Most are hunted down and killed.

Date	Event
September 20, 1943	Rome is occupied by Germans.
October 2, 1943	Hitler orders the deportation of the Jews of Denmark to Auschwitz. The Danes organize a massive rescue operation and more than 7,000 Jews are rescued and taken to Sweden. Only 477 Danish Jews were captured by the SS.
March 19, 1944	After their Hungarian ally tries to negotiate for peace with the Allies, the Germans invade and occupy Hungary. This sets the stage for the deportation of Hungarian Jews to Auschwitz.
May 15, 1944	Under the direction of Adolf Eichmann, Hungarian police and German SS begin to deport the Jews of Hungary even as the Red Army approaches. An estimated 465,000 were sent to Auschwitz by July. Most went directly to gas chambers.
October 31, 1944	Final transport of 14,000 Jews arrives at Auschwitz from Slovakia.
January 17, 1945	As the Red Army approaches, the Germans order 58,000 prisoners at Auschwitz onto the roads and begin the Death Marches to concentration camps in Germany. About 20,000 people died on the marches.
April 20, 1945	Hitler commits suicide.
May 8, 1945	Germany surrenders.

NAZI LEADERS AND DEPARTMENTS OF THE SS

The SS was not a single agency. It was made up of many different departments that were meant to control every aspect of life under German rule. The Main Office of the SS (RSHA) was directed by Reinhard Heydrich. With orders from Heinrich Himmler and using his own expert organizational talents, Heydrich created this enormous organization in 1938.

Agencies: *Gestapo*—Secret State Police
SD Inland—Secret Intelligence Service (within Germany)
SD Foreign—Secret Intelligence (occupied countries)
Kripo—Criminal Police
Ideology
Organization and Law

Each of these departments had several sub-departments. SD Foreign, for example, included the *Einsatzgruppen* (mobile killing units). The *Gestapo's* 15 sub-departments included: "Enemies" with a series of sub-categories: Communism, Sabotage, Liberalism, Assassinations. The next department, Department IV, was "Sects" and included Catholicism, Protestantism, Freemasonry, and Department IV B 4—Evacuations and Jews, headed by Adolf Eichmann.

Included in the RSHA was the administration of the death camps (not concentration camps) and the various national security and secret service organizations. The SS had grown to an enormous size with a bureaucracy that was almost unmanageable.

Separate from the RSHA were the divisions of the *Waffen SS,* the armed forces of the SS that fought in the war. These included the "Death's Head Division" and the "Adolf Hitler Division." The *Waffen SS* were crack troops, trained to fight to the death. There were height requirements for joining these divisions, and each person who enlisted had to produce written proof of his "Aryan" ancestry.

The SS was a rival of the *Wehrmacht,* the regular army. The SS troops were indoctrinated with Nazi ideas and usually were merciless when they dealt with "enemies of the *Reich,*" especially Jews. The *Wehrmacht,* although they cooperated with the *Einsatzgruppen,* tended to be less brutal when they were given tasks involving Jews.

At the Nuremberg Trials, the SD, the SS and the Gestapo were three organizations accused of war crimes and crimes against humanity. By 1941, the SS had more than four million members.

LIST OF NAZI LEADERS

1. **Adolf Eichmann:** Chief of "Evacuation and Jews" sector of the RSHA (Main SS Office). Responsible for organizing and directing deportation trains and deciding who would be on them. He escaped in 1945, was caught, tried and hanged in Jerusalem in 1961.

2. **Hans Frank:** Governor General of occupied Poland. Executed at Nuremberg in 1945.

3. **Paul Josef Goebbels:** Minister of Propaganda. Responsible for instigating and probably planning the events of the *Kristallnacht.* He committed suicide in Berlin in 1945.

4. **Hermann Goering:** Deputy *Fuehrer.* Second most powerful man in the Third *Reich;* director of the civil service, business and industry administration, and Field Marshall in charge of the Air Force. He committed suicide in his cell after being condemned to death by the International Military Tribunal at Nuremberg in 1945.

5. **Reinhard Heydrich:** Chief of the Main Office of the SS. Responsible only to Himmler and Hitler, he organized and put into action the "Final Solution." He was assassinated by Czech patriots in 1942.

6. **Heinrich Himmler:** Leader of the SS and Chief of German Police. Responsible only to Hitler, Himmler's forces, which included the dreaded *Gestapo* (Secret State Police), organized, administered and directed the murder of the Jews. He committed suicide after his capture in 1945.

7. **Rudolph Hoess:** Commandant of Auschwitz. He organized the three enormous camps at Auschwitz and supervised the gassing and murder of more than two million Jews. Hoess was executed at Auschwitz in 1947, hung on a gallows in the camp he had administered.

8. **Josef Mengele:** Physician in charge of the "selections" at Auschwitz. Mengele and his staff determined whether people would live or die. If people seemed strong enough for labor or somehow fit into a horrible medical experiment, Mengele allowed them to live for a period of time. Not only did he make such selections upon the arrival of the Jews, but also regularly checked prisoners in their barracks to eliminate those who were no longer "useful." Mengele escaped in 1945 and was given refuge in South America. In 1985, it was discovered that he had drowned in 1979.

VIDEO TEXT: LESSON 1

In 1920, approximately nine million Jews lived in Europe. In 1945, less than two million remained there. Six million had been murdered. Of those six million, one and a half million had been children under 15. The voices on this tape are of victims of the Holocaust who survived. Some lived through labor camps where they were forced to do slave labor; some survived death camps like Auschwitz {Owshvitz}. Others survived in hiding, constantly alert to the possibilities of betrayal or detection.

To each of them, the Holocaust means one fundamental fact: their families were annihilated. Jewish culture, whether in large cities or small towns, in France or Poland, revolved around close, tradition-oriented large families. Rich or poor, educated or not, their lives were directed by their religion, learning, work and community. In 1945, all of that was gone. Each of these people had lost from 40 to 80 family members.

Such terrible losses, made even worse by the way mothers, fathers, sisters and brothers were killed, have left their mark on the survivors.

This unit is, in part, about those victims and what the Holocaust means in very personal terms. It is also about the people who were responsible for that event. We might ask about the results it has had on these people. Has it changed their lives? Are they remorseful? Who are they and what were their tasks before and during the Holocaust?

Finally, because the Holocaust occurred so recently in the Western, civilized world, it has changed the ways in which many people think about that world. The lessons of this history might teach us how to avoid becoming victims, and, perhaps more importantly, how to avoid becoming perpetrators.

Let us first hear the voices of victims to better understand why this unit is so important. All the speakers are from the Detroit metropolitan area. All of them were between the ages of 14 and 16 when they experienced the Holocaust.

Their testimonies show us what the Holocaust was: the violent separation of children from their parents and families, the loss of home and protection, of security and warmth.

VIDEO TEXT: LESSON 8

The destruction of the European Jews has been called a "process." That means it proceeded in stages or steps. Each step seemed to make the next one possible. A governmental process needed the integration of civil service departments, the cooperation and work of offices that thought up, wrote and rewrote anti-Jewish directives and laws.

The members of different departments were given the tasks of devising the most efficient ways to put their orders into action. They received instructions, acted upon them and then passed the tasks on to the next department. The paperwork left their desks and was forgotten. But the results of their labor were devastating. This paperwork, these directives, uprooted communities, tore families apart, and brought death to innocent victims of all ages.

From April 1933, a torrent of anti-Jewish laws was passed in Germany. Jews were expelled from government civil service jobs; Jews were prohibited from becoming lawyers; Jewish children were prohibited from attending schools; Jewish university students were expelled; Jews could not hire non-Jews; Jews were dismissed from jobs in department stores and other types of businesses; Jews could not fly the German flag; Jews could not marry non-Jews; Jewish doctors could only treat Jewish patients.

In 1938 Jewish businesses were confiscated; eventually, food was rationed, curfews were imposed, and Jews were forced to live in specific areas and wear the Star of David whenever they were on the street. All this proved to be only the beginning of persecution that would assume unimaginable proportions.

The nationwide pogrom known as the *Kristallnacht* {*Kristall-nacht*} broke this systematic process. Jewish homes and businesses were smashed and looted. Jews were beaten in the streets. Twenty-six thousand Jews were arrested and placed in so-called "Protective Custody" in concentration camps.

Such violence, however, had the effect of angering many Germans who were willing to turn their backs on anti-Jewish laws and state-ordained discrimination but were offended by the open violence of the *Kristallnacht*.

After 1938, under the administrative guidance of Hermann Goering {*Hair-mann Ger-ring*}, Heinrich Himmler {*Hynerick Himmler*}, and Reynhard Heydrich {*Rinehard Hy-dritch*}, the "Solution to the Jewish Question" would return to the process of legal, orderly and systematic persecution. The police were under the direction of Himmler and his SS.

The courts were committed to enforcing the laws passed by the government. And the goal was to separate Jews from the rest of German society, then to isolate them and remove them from the country. This meant concentrating Jews in specific areas. The same policy would be pursued in Poland after September 1939, when Germany invaded that country.

In 1939, before the "Final Solution" of killing was planned, Heydrich and Himmler had decided to concentrate Jews in urban areas known as ghettos. For the German administrators, this plan presented a host of problems to be solved with expertise and efficiency. Jews who lived in large cities like Warsaw or Lodz {Luhdge} had to leave their homes and move into run-down neighborhoods.

Jews in small towns and villages were rounded up and brought to the newly formed ghettos. The property of Jews was to be confiscated. Areas had to be selected and cordoned off.

A system of governing the ghettos had to be devised. Guards had to be chosen. Rationing, curfews, labor details, all had to be worked out. Even the specific measurements of armbands with Stars of David on them had to be decreed. All this was done according to concise directions sent through the German bureaucracy in memoranda and orders. All this was set in motion because of a few written paragraphs.

Some 500,000 people died in the ghettos of eastern Europe from 1939 to mid-1944. Some of the victims who survived remember frightening details of the violence of the *Kristallnacht.* Others recall in very specific human terms the consequences of indifferently written orders for ghettos.

VIDEO TEXT: LESSON 10

His father was a private tutor for the son of the Duke of Bavaria. His uncle was a Catholic bishop. He was raised in the Catholic faith. He was an obedient and cautious child brought up in a strict but educated German home. After World War I, in which he was too young to serve, he went to school and hoped to study farming. Perhaps he would own a chicken farm some day, or be a teacher like his father.

He also dreamed about adventures in secret service agencies—fantasizing a leadership role in organizing an efficient police system. His quiet manner, studious ways and meticulous concern for details would lead him to some "suitable profession." Those who knew him admired his business-like precision, "disciplined obedience," his piety and devotion to his family and, later, to his men. One American who met him in the 1930s said of him: "I am convinced that nobody I met in Germany is more normal."

His name was Heinrich Himmler.

Heinrich Himmler became the *Reichsfuehrer* {*Reichs-Furor*} des *SS,* Leader of the SS, and Chief of German Police. He was accountable only to Hitler and was in charge of the destruction of the European Jews and responsible for almost every aspect of their annihilation. Himmler authorized the *Einsatzgruppen* {*Ein-zotz-grew-pen*} and the death camps. The six million murdered Jews were killed under his jurisdiction.

An obedient young child brought up in a strict Catholic home, this young man both feared and respected his father. As a teenager, he considered the priesthood but decided it would not be for him. In high school, his teachers thought he was not exceptionally bright but better than average. He had a talent for careful observation and organizing his work.

As a soldier in World War I, he became extremely patriotic and later was deeply depressed because of Germany's loss in that war. Times were hard, but his education provided him with skills, and his beloved wife and family gave him incentive to try different professions.

He seemed to feel a need for order and stability, a need he shared with most people of his generation. He had a simple, uncritical mind and struck people as uninvolved and cold. He said of himself that he was able to follow orders without thinking about them—a good employee. An excellent organizer, he became famous for his attention to the smallest details and his ability to focus on technical questions and to solve technical problems. He remained devout and rigid. All in all, an average citizen.

His name was Rudolf Hoess {*Hess*}.

Rudolph Hoess became the Commandant of Auschwitz. Commissioned by Himmler in 1941, he organized the procedures that resulted in the death of more than two million Jews by gassing, shooting, starvation, medical experiments, beatings or disease.

Born in Germany, he was raised in Linz, Austria. His father was a bookkeeper for an electric company. After he did poorly in a technical high school, his father found him a job with the electric company. Having failed in school and then at his new job, he was given another, at the urging of his father. After this brief work, he began selling vacuum cleaners but was soon released from this position.

He moved to Germany, as a German citizen, in search of work and a better life—perhaps with a family. It was 1933. He admired and even envied those few friends he had made who were aristocrats with titles, and followed them wherever he could. He was helpful, attentive, a follower who obeyed authority figures—from his father to older friends. To this point in his life, he was a rather mediocre person.

His name was Adolf Eichmann.

Adolph Eichmann became Chief of the Office of Evacuation and Jews in the Security Service section of the SS. His first task was to deport the Jews of Austria, and he devised assembly-line methods for efficient deportation. His last task was the deportation of almost one-half million Jews from Hungary to Auschwitz in 1944. He achieved great success in both tasks. He was responsible for the deportation and murder of more than one million Jews.

He was the son of a famous director of a music conservatory. By the time this man was 18, he had distinguished himself as a student and a musician. He could have chosen a career as an academic or a violinist. Brilliant in school, he excelled in fencing and other athletics. His mother was a devout Catholic and raised him in the Catholic faith, and his musical abilities did not keep his parents from sending him to a strict boys school.

He was alert, energetic, hard-working and rigid. He was coldly handsome, the model "Aryan" {Air-ee-an}. Ambitious and determined, his clear and calculating mind brought him the reputation of being able to solve any technical or organizational problem.

Some called him an opportunist. Others saw him as a perfectionist. He was objective and unemotional. He continued to play Bach violin sonatas. He was unique among his peers.

His name was Reinhard Heydrich.

Reinhard Heydrich became the Chief of the Main Office of the SS. He coordinated all the many operations of the SS. In 1939, Heydrich was put in charge of organizing the "Final Solution." He was directly responsible, before his assassination in 1942, for establishing all the procedures that led to the murder of two million Jews up until 1942. His methods and procedures were also used in the murder of four million more Jews between 1943 and 1945.

VIDEO TEXT: LESSON 13

On October 15, 1941, Hans Frank {Hahns Frahnk}, the Nazi Governor General of occupied Poland, issued a public order imposing the death penalty on persons hiding Jews outside the ghettos. The threat of death was not empty rhetoric, as Poles and Germans in that area knew. Punishments for even the slightest aid to Jews were quick and brutal, often public, and took the form of shooting or hanging or imprisonment in a concentration camp. There were non-Jews, however, who acted humanely, breaking the law to hide, rescue or somehow help Jews.

In the midst of indifference, apathy and collaboration, there were examples of courageous and righteous behavior. In Amsterdam, although most were eventually caught and killed, approximately 25,000 Jews were hidden at one time or another.

Among them were the young Anne Frank and her family. The four people who chose to hide the Franks did so knowing they were endangering the lives of their friends and families. Yet, they took the risk. To offer assistance was not a simple act of moral conviction—it involved painful decisions about jeopardizing family members.

The Nazi system of collective responsibility—making a group responsible for the actions of one person—made offering assistance doubly difficult. Those who offered aid and rescued Jews were heroes; yet, they often saw themselves as potentially responsible for the death of innocent members of their families. Moral action was not a simple choice—it might simultaneously produce deadly consequences.

Perhaps the most instructive story of rescue is the Danish one. Denmark was occupied by the Germans in 1940. In 1943, SS headquarters in Berlin sent orders to the SS in Denmark demanding that all Jews in Denmark be rounded up for deportation to Auschwitz. The Danish police and the Danish civil service refused to cooperate with the SS.

When the Germans moved to round up the Jews of Denmark, the Danish population worked together to rescue over 7,000 Jews by sending them in boats to Sweden where they were offered refuge. The Danes, as a nation, acted heroically. In the small town of LeChambon {Le-Shombon} in Southern France, the citizens hid Jews who managed to get there. The people of LeChambon then escorted the Jews under cover of night to Switzerland where they were smuggled across the border to safety. The people of LeChambon, as a group, acted heroically.

There were many individuals who offered to hide Jews. Jews were hidden in every European city—Warsaw, Budapest, Paris, Berlin, Amsterdam and others. In the rural areas of every country, farmers hid Jews in their barns or cellars. Some clergymen hid Jews in churches and monasteries. Members of the underground prepared false identity papers for Jews. The people on this tape survived by hiding or running from one place to another. Like them, almost all who survived needed some help from someone at some time.

Perhaps one should devote time to studying the Danes, examining the motives of the people of LeChambon and the would-be rescuers of the Frank family. For all of them, life was sacred. Hope lies with the rescuers—there were pitifully too few of them.

ADDITIONAL ACTIVITIES

The following films complement the curriculum:

☐ "The Avenue of the Just" (55 minutes). Refers to the tree-lined walk at the Yad Vashem memorial museum in Israel, which honors the rescuers of Jews during the Holocaust. The film is about ten of those heroic individuals and includes interviews with some of them and some of those who were rescued. Among those interviewed are Anne Frank's father and the people who hid the Frank family in Amsterdam. (Lessons 13 or 14)

Anti-Defamation League of B'nai B'rith, rental fee $40.

☐ "The Camera of My Family" (18 minutes). A film about tracing the history of a German Jewish family through original photographs. Well-integrated historical material with personal family history. Very poignant.

Anti-Defamation League of the B'nai B'rith, rental fee $20.

☐ "The Courage to Care" (27 minutes). A film about those who helped rescue Jews. Features interviews with Elie Wiesel, several Jews who were hidden and those who were responsible for saving lives during the Holocaust. Moving and sensitively done. Nominated for an Academy Award in 1985.

Anti-Defamation League of the B'nai B'rith.

☐ "Denmark '43" (22 minutes). A film about the successful Danish rescue of the Jews in Denmark. A present-day Danish high school teacher has his students reenact—on location— the courageous rescue in a fishing village. Excellent photography and music. (Lesson 13)

Jewish Media Service, rental fee $20.

☐ "Genocide." A feature film narrated by Orson Welles and Elizabeth Taylor. The history of the Holocaust in pictures and film. Includes comments by Simon Wiesenthal, famed Nazi hunter and founder of the Simon Wiesenthal Center. (Any lesson after Lesson 10)

Simon Wiesenthal Center.

☐ "The Hangman" (12 minutes). Pass out and discuss the poem, "The Hangman" by Maurice Ogden. This animated parable tells the story of the people of a town who are condemned to be hanged, one by one, by a mysterious stranger who erects an ominous gallows in the center of the town. For each hanging, the remaining townspeople find a rationale—from fear, prejudice or indifference. The last survivor finds that the rope has been meant for "he who serves me best": the person who has failed to speak out and now finds that no one is left to speak out for him. Good companion to Martin Niemoeller's statement in Student booklet, Reading 2C. (Lesson 2)

Jewish Media Service, rental fee $25.

☐ "I Never Saw Another Butterfly" (15 minutes). Adaptation of the book of children's drawings and poems from the Theresienstadt concentration camp. Good mood piece with sensitive music sung by a children's choir. (Lessons 9-12 or 17 and 18)

Board of Jewish Education, New York, rental fee, $10.

☐ "Joseph Schultz" (13 minutes). True story about a German soldier who, after taking part in the destruction of a small Yugoslav village, refuses to join the firing squad execution of all the men of the village. He quietly joined the victims and was shot with them. (Lesson 13)

Jewish Media Service, rental fee $17.

☐ "Memorandum" (58 minutes). This film integrates several different events that occurred in 1964: a pilgrimage of survivors to Bergen-Belsen who return along with the British commanding officer of the liberation of Bergen-Belsen; the judgment day at the trial of 20 Auschwitz personnel; the opening of the play about the Auschwitz trials, "The Investigation." Raises questions about who was responsible for the murder of the Jews, why it is important to remember "who murdered by memorandum?," and others. (Lesson 10)

Anti-Defamation League, rental fee $30.

☐ "Night and Fog" (31 minutes). French film about the concentration and death camps. One of the finest documentaries made on the Holocaust; "brutally graphic" with jarring music and a darkly poetic narrative by French poet-survivor Jean Cayrol. Director Alain Resnais deliberately juxtaposed haunting scenes of the camps as they are today, in bright color, with the black and white documentary footage of the 1940s. The contrast is shocking and eerie. While there is no special emphasis on Jews, it nevertheless is clearly about the murder of the Jews. (Any lesson after Lesson 10)

Films, Inc., rental fee $55.

☐ "Sosua" (30 minutes). A film about a community established in the Dominican Republic during the Holocaust as a haven for Jewish refugees. Contains scenes of the Evian Conference and the early days of Sosua. An unusual and unique story. (Lesson 16)

Sosua-Sol Productions, Inc., rental fee $50.

☐ "Verdict for Tomorrow" (28 minutes). Analysis of the Eichmann trial in Jerusalem in 1961. Contains excerpts from the trial and commentary and narration by Lowell Thomas. (Lesson 17)

Anti-Defamation League of B'nai B'rith, rental fee $20.

☐ "The Warsaw Ghetto" (51 minutes). Fine documentary of the history of the ghetto and the uprising. Narrated by a survivor of the ghetto, it documents the persecution and murder of the Jews in Warsaw. The film is compiled of Nazi photographs, propaganda pictures and other records. In contrast to the atrocities is the humanity of the narrator and the victims' attempt to maintain human dignity. (Any lesson after Lesson 8; also Lesson 15)

Anti-Defamation League of B'nai B'rith, rental fee $30.

HOLOCAUST EDUCATION AND MEMORIAL CENTERS

A trip to a Holocaust museum or educational center is recommended if there is one in the area. This activity should follow Lesson 10.

California

Fullerton

The Holocaust Archives: In the library of California State University. A collection of letters, documents, diaries, poetry, music and mementoes of the Nazi concentration camps and death camps. Also contains taped interviews with survivors.

Los Angeles

Martyrs Memorial for Jewish Federation-Council: Located on the twelfth floor of the Jewish Community Building, 6505 Wilshire Boulevard. The official Yad Vashem memorial in Los Angeles. A dramatic museum for the purpose of memorializing the victims killed by the Nazis. The museum also contains original documents, photographs and artifacts.

Simon Wiesenthal Center for Holocaust Studies: At Yeshiva University, 9760 West Pico Boulevard. Named after the famous Nazi hunter. The Center includes a library, commemoration hall, lecture area, multi-media complex and exhibits depicting the rise and fall of Nazism, European Jewry, leading Nazis and recent events regarding human rights denial.

San Francisco

Holocaust Library and Research Center, 601 14th Avenue. Houses a collection of some 5,000 books in various languages and a collection of documents.

Florida

Southeastern Florida Holocaust Memorial Center: Bay Vista Campus—Florida International University. Includes collections of oral histories and educational material.

Illinois

Chicago

Bernard and Rochelle Zell Holocaust Memorial, Spertus College, 612 Michigan Avenue: Museum contains artifacts, literature, photographs and an audiovisual component.

Maryland
Baltimore

Aaron H. Leibtag Resource Center in the Board of Jewish Education Building, 5800 Park Heights Avenue: Contains artifacts, documents and other resources as well as changing exhibits on the Holocaust.

Michigan
West Bloomfield

Holocaust Memorial Center, 6600 West Maple, adjacent to the Jewish Community Center: Museum and resource center includes a library, audiovisual exhibits, videotaped and audiotaped survivor testimonies, artifacts and photographs.

New York
Binghamton

The Margolis Holocaust Collection at the State University of New York, Binghamton: Contains books, documents and other materials.

Brooklyn

The Center for Holocaust Studies, 1609 Avenue J: Contains oral histories, slides, movies, diaries, letters, photographs and artifacts.

Canada
Montreal

The Montreal Holocaust Memorial, Allied Jewish Community Services' Cummings House, 5151 Cote Sainte Catherine Road: Educational resource center containing exhibit of artifacts and graphics as well as rotating exhibits and public programs. Also contains audiovisual material.

A SELECT, ANNOTATED BIBLIOGRAPHY

History

Bauer, Yehuda. *A History of the Holocaust.* A concise and straightforward historical account. It includes much material on Jewish resistance and non-Jewish rescue attempts and good chapters on pre-war Europe.

Bullock, Allan. *Hitler: A Study in Tyranny.* Perhaps the best general biography of Hitler and the rise of Nazism.

Dawidowicz, Lucy. *A Holocaust Reader.* Excellent collection of original documents grouped according to pre-1933, 1933-38, 1939-45. Includes excerpts from diaries of German Jews, ghetto victims and resistance fighters as well as SS memoranda, speeches and legislation.

Fest, Joachim. *The Face of the Third Reich.* Good collection of biographical portraits of the Nazi leaders. Includes Hitler, Himmler, Heydrich, Goering and others.

Gay, Peter. *Weimar Culture.* Best essay on the culture of the Weimar Republic.

Gilbert, G. M. *Nuremberg Diary.* Written by the psychiatrist who examined and regularly met with the 21 defendants of the Nuremberg War Crimes Trial.

Gilbert, Martin. *Auschwitz and the Allies.* The story of the Allies' refusal to come to the aid of the victims during World War II.

Gilbert, Martin. *A Holocaust Atlas.* Indispensable collection of maps.

Hilberg, Raul. *The Destruction of the European Jews.* Definitive history of the murder of the Jews of Europe. The student edition has been revised and omits large sections from the original edition, which has now appeared in three volumes.

Hilberg, Staron, Kermisz, eds. *The Warsaw Diary of Adam Czerniakow.* Perhaps the most important of the many personal memoirs, this diary was kept by the head of the Jewish Council until his suicide in June 1942.

Lanzmann, Claude. *Shoah: An Oral History of the Holocaust.* The text of the remarkable 9½ hour movie. Included are interviews with Polish peasants and railroad workers, German officials and railroad bureaucrats, as well as with Jan Karski and Raul Hilberg and many survivors.

Laqueur, Walter. *The Terrible Secret.* The surprising story of the Allied governments' refusal to help the Jews of Europe.

Levi, Primo. *Survival In Auschwitz.* Excellent, brief personal account of life in Auschwitz by a brilliant Italian Jewish writer.

Lifton, Robert J. *The Nazi Doctors.* Outstanding (if long) study of the participation of the medical profession in the Holocaust.

Morse, Arthur D. *While Six Million Died.* Startling revelation of the lack of concern shown by American officials to the plight of the Jews.

Novitch, Miriam. *Sobibor.* History of the death camp until its destruction in 1943.

Reitlinger, Gerald. *The SS: Alibi of a Nation.* One of the earliest and best histories of the SS.

Serenyi, Gita. *Into That Darkness.* Chilling series of interviews with Franz Stangl, former commandant of Treblinka.

Wheaton, I. *The Nazi Revolution, 1933-1935: Prelude to Calamity.* Very detailed, day-by-day history of events.

Wyman, David. *The Abandonment of the Jews.* Follows the same thesis of Arthur Morse (above) but more thoroughly documented.

Literature and Personal Memoirs

Borowski, Thaddeus. *This Way for the Gas, Ladies and Gentlemen.* Excellent but horrifying collection of short stories by a non-Jewish survivor of Auschwitz.

Delbo, Charlotte. *None of Them Shall Return.* Moving collection of dramatic poems by a French survivor

Hart, Kitty. *Return to Auschwitz: The Remarkable Story of a Girl Who Survived the Holocaust.* Autobiographical account of a French Jew who survived in hiding and then in Auschwitz. Vivid portrait of the daily routine at Auschwitz.

Hillesum, Etty. *An Interrupted Life: the Diaries of Etty Hillesum, 1941-1943.* Excerpts from the diaries of a young Dutch Jewish woman who was sent to Auschwitz at age 27.